"One of the greatest living American writers."
—*The Dallas Observer*

"An Olympian mastery of language."
—*Library Journal*

"Blindingly brilliant."
—*Entertainment Weekly*

"There are, in fact, very few writers who have Nick Tosches' singular gift."
—*David Hare, The Spectator*

"Tosches works wonders."
—*The Los Angeles Herald Examiner*

"Nick Tosches is a beautiful thug [who] has always beaten back a demon while inhabiting the very soul of the beast."
—*Philadelphia City Paper*

"The story-teller of hell."
—*L'Officiel Homme*

"Nick Tosches's pen is a knife that can whittle anything well!"
—*Alexander Theroux*

"After all, the guy's from Jersey, with the rest of us mobsters."
—*Amiri Baraka*

OTHER BOOKS BY
NICK TOSCHES

Country

Hellfire

Unsung Heroes of Rock 'n' Roll

Frankie, Parts 1 and 2
(with Richard Meltzer)

Power on Earth

Cut Numbers

Dino

Trinities

Chaldea / I Dig Girls

The Devil and Sonny Liston

The Nick Tosches Reader

Where Dead Voices Gather

The Last Opium Den

In the Hand of Dante

King of the Jews

Never Trust a Loving God
(with Thierry Alonso Gravleur)

SAVE THE LAST DANCE FOR SATAN

by
Nick Tosches

KICKS BOOKS
NEW YORK, NEW YORK

Copyright © 2011 by Nick Tosches, Inc.

Much of the contents of this book was first published, as "Hipsters and Hoodlums," in Vanity Fair No. 484, December 2000.

All rights reserved. No part of this book may be reproduced in any form or by any electronic or mechanical means, including information and retrieval systems, without permission in writing from the publisher, except by a reviewer who may quote brief passages in a review.

Published in 2011 by Kicks Books
An imprint of Kicks Magazine
PO Box 646 Cooper Station
New York NY 10276

Printed in the United States of America

Second Printing 2012
Hurricane Sandy Edition

ISBN: 978-0-9659777-3-9

Editor: Miriam Linna
Design: Patrick Broderick/Rotodesign

www.kicksbooks.com

First Edition

IN MEMORIAM
BIG BARNEY BAKER
WHO HEARD MUCH, TOLD LITTLE

ACKNOWLEDGEMENTS

Jerry Blavat and Freddy DeMann are to be thanked for encouraging me to write the original story from which this little book grew. That story was first published, as "Hipsters and Hoodlums," in the December 2000 issue of *Vanity Fair*, for which Graydon Carter and others at that magazine are to be thanked. Just as I had long wanted to tell the story—probably as far back as 1978, when I met and wrote about the song-plugger Juggy Gayles, whose memory must also be acknowledged—so for a decade after I told it did I want to revise and expand it into a modest volume of its own; and Miriam Linna is to be thanked for encouraging me to do so, and for bringing it out as the third in her small but growing and distinguished series.

I should like to thank all those whose participation in the story is the true life of the story, from Jerry and Freddy to Carmine "Wassel" De Noia and Hy Weiss. I was sorry to hear of Hy's passing in March of 2007. The likes of him won't come this way again.

For their help in the writing of the long section on the Jaynetts and "Sally, Go 'Round the Roses" for the present edition, the following are to be thanked: Artie Butler, Al Gorgoni, Sally Nordlund, Buddy Resnik, and especially Louise Harris and

Lezli Valentine, formerly of the Jaynetts who recorded "Sally." Much research material for this section, as well as for the new section on Jack Ruby, was provided by Miriam Linna.

Others who contributed to this book include Debra Catanzaro, Cami Dreyer, Bob Merlis, Billy Miller, Michael Pietsch, Abby Royle, Gene Sculatti, Joe Smith, the late Jerry Wexler, Peter Wolf, and one who wishes to remain unnamed.

*Coins clinking into
the big incandescent
Bakelite jukebox.
Coins showering to
the street from a
ninth-story window.
Yes, it was a time.*

SAVE THE LAST DANCE FOR SATAN

by

NICK TOSCHES

ONE

It was a time, all right.

"So, anyway, this character, this punk of a disc jockey from Chicago, ends up working here in New York. We have this record, nice little record. We need to break out the record. This is back in 1962 or so. It was pay for play. That's what promotion was all about. A hundred, a few hundred bucks. Five hundred, a thousand copies of the record that they could take down to the store to sell.

"So this disc jockey, he's like a midget, this guy, about four and a half feet high, I guess he figures he's a big shot. He takes the money, but he don't play the record. What he does, he goes on the air, says, 'I'm about to break this new record.' And then he breaks it—I mean, *breaks* it; cracks it into pieces—says, 'I wouldn't play this record if my mother gave it to me.' Like I say, I guess this little prick thinks he's something. Maybe all that candy-ass Chicago tough-guy shit went to his head. Anyway, he wasn't in Chicago no more. This was New York."

It was said that Hyman Weiss, the Romanian-born Jew who had founded Old Town Records in the cloakroom of the Triboro Theatre in Harlem in 1954, chose to call his label by that name because his brother and partner, Sam Weiss, had been working for a Brooklyn paper company called Old Town and had a lot of stationery bearing that name.

Hymie remembers his first act as "a guy named Cherokee." He remembers that he sold this Cherokee guy "a car that wouldn't start unless you pushed it downhill."

Old Town survived through black doo-wop groups, such as the Solitaires, who achieved local success in the Northeastern golden triangle of New York-Newark-Philadelphia, and would later prosper with national hit records by Arthur Prysock—Hy's favorite—and the Earls, a white doo-wop group from the Bronx. Within a year of Old Town's inception, Hy moved into a real office, down on Seventh Avenue, and by 1958 he was operating out of 1697 Broadway, later known as the Ed Sullivan Theater building, just up the road from the cathedral of the music business, the Brill Building, at 1619 Broadway, at the southwest corner of Forty-ninth Street.

After the Chicago disc jockey's act of insolence, Hy Weiss arranged a meeting at the Old Town office, which was on the ninth floor. The record wasn't Hy's; he was only acting as an intermediary for the aggrieved parties. Also present was Carmine De Noia, a Broadway bookmaker who was a friend of those in the music business.

Carmine was an imposing man. His friends called him Wassel, after the manner in which he strode, carrying his prodigious weight in what was neither quite waddle nor hustle, but *wassel*. Another story had it that Wassel's nickname was derived from the way he had pronounced the word "rascal" as a boy.

His father, also named Carmine De Noia and known as Jardine, was a prodigious eater who served as the inspiration for the character of the Broadway glutton Nicely-Nicely Jones in the 1931 Damon Runyon short-story collection *Guys and Dolls*.

"I used to help them," Wassel says, not much less imposing today—the year is A.D. 2000—at seventy-nine, than he was in the old days. "See, I was the only Italian guy on Broadway, and I didn't take no crap from nobody. I respected everybody, but nobody would fool with me because I would never rob anybody.

"Hy goes into the other room," says Wassel with a laugh, his memory wandering back over forty years, his voice deep, sonorous, and disarmingly blithe. "So here's this disc jockey. And I'm looking at him, and he's, like, this little midget. I throw open the window, pick him up, flip him, shake him out by the ankles. Ninth floor. All the change fell out of his pockets. Some friends of mine picked it up."

The disc jockey played the record during his next broadcast, and he kept playing it. Soon, however, he was back in Chicago.

"He denied it ever happened," Wassel says. "Some guys asked him. He denied it. I said, 'Let him deny it. That's all right. Let him deny it.'"

"See," says another old-timer, "it wasn't that this guy didn't want to play the record. It was that he took the money, *then* didn't play the record. He wasn't a stand-up guy."

"Same thing as today, lot of fakers."

"Yeah," says Wassel. "I remember, there was this song I liked"—the song was "All Right, OK, You Win," recorded in 1955 by Ella Johnson, who sang in the rhythm-and-blues band of her brother Buddy Johnson—"and Sid Weiss"—a songwriter, no relation to Hy—"gave the publishing on it to me. So what am I gonna do with it now? Am I gonna put it on the wall? I don't know anything about publishing."

Wassel got a telephone call from a song publisher whose name is lost to the years.

"Your name Wassel?"

"Yeah."

"You got a song we want."

"I don't want no trouble."

"We want the song."

Wassel wrapped a length of pipe in a rolled-up newspaper. "I went up there, and the guy was a nasty guy. If he would've talked nice to me, I would've gave it to him. I didn't care; I didn't know anything about publishing. So, anyway, I went up there. This guy's sitting at his desk with his feet on the desk.

"Listen," said Wassel, "what do you want?"

"You know what I want. Just put the song over there."

Wassel looked at him. "I says, 'Here.' I came down with the pipe. I broke everything. The desk, everything."

Had the would-be wiseguy asked, he would have received. But, as Wassel says, "he was trying to shake me down."

Everybody was trying to shake down everybody. Among the Jews who ran the music business, it was treachery without end within the temple. "Every time guys came up to Hy Weiss's office, it was a shake-down. 'Hey, man, you got any bread.' I'd be there, I said, 'Look, this ain't no grocery store. I mean, this is a grocery store? It's not a grocery store.' One guy pulled a knife. I didn't care. I was wild then. But we were trying to make a living; that's all we wanted to do."

There was the day he was called up to the Brill Building office of Benny Goodman's music publishing company, which was run by a couple of dead Benny's brothers, Gene and Harry. A kid who was with the Fiestas, a group that recorded for Hy Weiss, was trying to get a long-overdue royalty statement from the brothers. The kid had one of them against the wall and was holding a broken Coca-Cola bottle to his throat when Wassel arrived.

"I took the broken Coke bottle from the kid, spiked it down like a shiv into the guy's desk. 'Send him his royalties.'"

Money, money, money—"Money Honey," as the Drifters sang in 1953—all the time, money.

When one young singer was owed, Wassel summoned the gonif who owed.

"I'll sit on it," the gonif said when Wassel proposed that the kid get his due.

"Listen, you Jew bastard, you sit on it, you're

gonna be sittin' on three holes."

"Why?"

"Because I'm gonna shoot you two new ones."

Yes, money, money, money.

There were record-counterfeiting operations to be dealt with. Wassel remembers four such jobs: one on Ditmars Boulevard in Astoria; one in Newark; one in Brooklyn; another locale forgotten.

"The Brooklyn job was something. They had this really vicious guard dog. So every day, I'd go by and feed it. Finally, I figure the dog likes me, I take my shot, go in with a few other guys, bust up the joint. We used to hang around waiting to get arrested. See, we had the evidence, all the pressing stuff we'd broken up, so we knew nobody would press charges, the case would be thrown right out."

Yes, money, money. But not always loot. Men such as Wassel in those days were paid as promotion men; and, as recalcitrant disc jockeys and others discovered the hard way, they were quite effective as such. But promotion also encompassed a wider and gentler, albeit often sub rosa, range of duties, not restricted to the milieu of the small, mongrel record companies. There was the time when Columbia, one of the biggest and most established of the major companies, called in an outside "promotion man" to trail a young man who, in his twenties, was among Columbia's most successful pop singers. Trailing him was a sort of undercover form of public-relations insurance.

I ask Wassel exactly what he means.

"You know. Make sure he steered clear of the *wrong* people, *wrong* places."

I still don't understand.

"You know."

I don't know. Was the singer consorting with the Mob?

I get a look that seems to say: I'm talking about wrong people, wrong places.

"They wanted to make sure nobody caught him with a dick in his mouth."

Hy Weiss, frail and gentle in his old age, had been a bouncer at a White Rose bar in his early years, and was himself sometimes occasionally called upon to aid a friend in promotion-related undertakings. There was a call one morning from a record man, who, with his wife, ran one of the premier R&B companies. The couple was having problems with a distributor with whom they had contracted to share space in their building on Tenth Avenue, and they could not get him out.

"You gotta meet me at seven in the morning,"

he says to Hy, meaning Saturday morning.

"O.K., what for?"

"When you get here."

"You sure it's important?"

"Absolutely."

Hy arrives early Saturday morning. There's the guy, and he's holding a big metal can.

"I got gas."

"What are you gonna do with this gas?"

"I'm gonna burn down the building."

A pause. "I don't cook on Saturday."

The Sabbath.

TWO

Wassel's elusive career in the undergrowth of the music business dated to the early fifties, during the golden age of rock and roll. He was, as he says, a bookmaker, taking action on horses among the Broadway crowd, of which the growing cast of characters in the burgeoning world of rock and roll were fast replacing and outnumbering the Tin Pan Alley veterans who had occupied the Brill Building since 1931.

"It didn't last very long," he says of his Broadway bookmaking days, which began in 1949. "I used to go to Jack Dempsey's to get a little action. I used to go to Lindy's, to Gallagher's."

These were the mythic places of old Broadway: Gallagher's, on West Fifty-second Street, which had begun as a speakeasy in 1927; Lindy's, on Broadway, just north of the Brill Building, a restaurant and hangout that operated round the clock, had been a hangout of Arnold Rothstein's, and was the "Mindy's" of Damon Runyon's tale-telling; Jack Dempsey's, which was located on the ground floor of the Brill Building. The Jewish entrepreneurs of the music business were inveterate gamblers: their success was built upon daring to venture into an untamed new territory—rock and roll—where the established, major companies feared to enter. But the gains of their business gambles were all too often lost to gambling of a more common kind; and it was through their betting that Wassel, during his short-lived career as a bookie, came to know them.

"He knew them because they were all booking through him," one of his friends says.

"That was how they all got in trouble. They gambled and they lost and they couldn't pay off. They shook each other down. But the Mob never shook them down. The Mob never came to them. They came to the Mob, because their gambling debts drove them to the Mob."

Aside from the partnerships of collateral interest pursuant to its role as rock and roll's lender of last resort, the Mob's primary involvement with rock and roll, as it had been for many years with the music business in general, was through the jukebox racket. Since 1946, exclusive licenses to sell Wurlitzer jukeboxes were held by the Emby Distributing Company. Located on West Forty-third Street, the Emby corporation was controlled by Frank Costello and Meyer Lansky, the two biggest gangsters in New York. Until recently, in certain quarters, one might still be urged to feed the jukebox with the wry words, "Play another record; their daughters need new Cadillacs."

Coins clinking into the big incandescent Bakelite jukebox. Coins showering to the street from a ninth-story window. Yes, it was a time.

THREE

It was a time of rock and roll's innocence—that is to say, its incarnation of innocence. The golden age of rock and roll can be said to have begun in 1945, when hip black urban music diverged into two distinct revolutionary currents: the more cerebral and Apollonian freshet of bebop, and the more febrile and Dionysian torrent of rhythm and blues, as pioneered by blues shouters of the day such as Wynonie Harris. That age would last for little more than a decade. Elvis Presley marked its end, and it was as if the golden age of real rock and roll had never been, as the all-powerful consumer mainstream of white America in its belated discovery of rock and roll knew only the banal Wonder Bread of its usurpation by the forces of market-friendly mediocrity.

This is not to say that the beast of rock and

roll had raged in sovereignty from World War II until the ascendance of Elvis. In 1951, the year of Jackie Brenston and His Delta Cats' "Rocket '88'," perhaps the first truly devastating rock and roll wrecking-ball to hit No. 1 in its demolition of the rhythm-and-blues charts, there were also far less feral manifestations of rock and roll that enjoyed even greater success: Amos Milburn's soft and fatalistic "Bad, Bad Whiskey," Charles Brown's haunting "Black Night." And while two of the raunchiest, rockingest vocal-group records, "Work with Me, Annie" and "Sexy Ways," both by Hank Ballard and the Midnighters, dated to the months before Elvis's first recordings, in 1954, the much more innocuous fare of doo-wop had by then come to define the New York vocal-group sound of the Brill Building's ever increasing dominion.

Moreover, white artists were recording insipid version of R&B hits from almost the outset, such as Frank Sinatra trying to revive a faltering career by covering "The Huckle-Buck" of 1949—a foreshadowing of the more heartfelt and expert mediocritizing of R&B that later would carry Elvis to fame.

As I chronicled in detail in the introduction to my book *Unsung Heroes of Rock and Roll*, the inchoate beast of rock and roll emerged in the middle of a war, when the world was mad and big-band swing was all the rage. As the summer of 1942 began, the outlook of the recording industry was bleak. Records were made of shellac, and the countries that were the major suppliers of shellac were blockaded. The shipping and distribution of records were becoming increasingly problematic, as the Office of Defense commandeered every means of transport. When the president of the American Federation of Musicians, James Caesar Petrillo, a crusader against "the menace of mechanical music," announced on June 25 that all recording licenses would be annulled on August 1 and would not be renewed until certain excessive demands were met, the industry felt as if it had received the kiss of death. Recording companies rushed to lay in enough new recordings to last them through the ban.

The ban lasted for more than a year, but it did not affect the industry the way the industry had feared it would. Nineteen forty-three turned out to be its most prosperous year in over a decade, as the problems it faced were more than offset by a record-buying public that wanted dearly to be distracted from the reality of war, and that had the prosperity to pay for that distraction. Big-band swing was still the rage. Benny Goodman, Harry James, Glenn Miller, and the Dorsey brothers were the men whose music dominated the early 1940's. Columbia, which had Goodman and James, Victor, which had Miller and Tommy Dorsey, and Decca, which had Jimmy Dorsey, were the three companies that dominated the industry.

But as the new music spread, and as it became obvious that the prospering major companies were for the most part unaware of and uninterested in the sea change, numerous little labels were founded by men and women who smelled money in what was happening. In 1942, during the A.F.M. ban, Herman Lubinsky started Savoy Records in downtown Newark. In Los Angeles, in 1944, the songwriter Otis René, Jr., started Excelsior ("The All Colored Recording Company"). In Harlem, in 1943, Ike and Bess Berman formed Apollo. The mongrel labels were a book of begats, a Fourth Book of Moses unto themselves—Exclusive and DeLuxe, National and King, Modern and Aladdin, Mercury and Specialty, Atlantic and Chess, Duke and Sun, Vee-Jay and Old Town, and hundreds more—and they were the true breeding-ground and glory-ground of rock and roll.

The industry establishment did not quite know what to make of the new music. By 1954, the major companies were paying for their sins. Looking askance for too long at rock and roll, regarding it as a passing fad that soon would pass, they began to see how much money they had been missing out on since the late forties. All the best-selling rock and roll hits, all the biggest artists, had belonged to those mongrel labels, some of which, such as Atlantic and Chess, were on their way to becoming major labels.

As 1955 began, the big old-line companies were trying desperately to cash in on rock and roll. Since they did not understand what rock and roll was, the maladroit rushing of their greed was marvelous to behold. Columbia decided that Tony Bennett would be its rock and roll star. "DIG THE CRAZIEST!! HE SWINGS!! HE ROCKS!! HE GOES!!" Bennett's "Close Your Eyes" was advertised as an "ASTOUNDING RHYTHM AND BLUES RENDITION." Needless to say, Tony didn't make it as a rock and roll star. RCA-Victor's proposal was more absurd. "DIG PERRY IN ACTION ON A GREAT 'ROCK-AND-ROLL' RECORD," implored the January 1955 ads for Perry Como's cover version of Gene & Eunice's "Ko Ko Mo," which was currently a hit on the mongrel Combo label. But by the end of the year, no one was laughing at RCA-Victor. If they couldn't make it, they would buy it: in late November, RCA-Victor bought Elvis Presley from Sam Phillips's little Sun Records of Memphis, and in 1956, with Elvis, RCA-Victor marked the beginning of the end not only of the golden age of untamed rock and roll, but of that age's mongrel labels as well. Those few that survived became major labels, or lingered on for a while, then were consumed or vanished; and a whole new wave of small labels, such as Jubilee and Roulette, came into being as the maverick masters of rock and roll's incarnation of innocence.

The ascendance of the pose of innocence could be traced to 1954, the year of Elvis's first records and of "Gee" by the Crows. Indeed, the Crows' record, which some consider, oddly, to be the first rock and roll hit—a misguided assertion based solely on the fact that, while other records had crossed over from the R&B to the pop charts, "Gee," in the spring of 1954, broke simultaneously on both charts—was about as sweet and innocent as it got. If anything, "Gee," like Elvis, was the sunset of one age and the dawning of another: the first hit not of rock and roll, but of rock and roll's silver age, the age of its rebirth, like a virgin, to sing its songs of money-making innocence beneath the windows of a new and innocent generation. From rotgut to milkshakes, do-rags to ponytails. In 1950, Wynonie Harris had pulled off a joyous Top 10 R&B hit about running wild with a fifteen-year-old girl. In 1957—the year the Everly Brothers hit No. 1 on both the R&B and pop charts with "Wake Up Little Susie," a song about the anticipation of parental reprimand when curfew is violated by dozing off chastely during a date—Andre Williams, hanging tough and true to the spirit, could not even find a breach at the bottom of the R&B charts with his "Jail Bait." The following year, however, embracing the new antithetical ethos of innocence, Chuck Berry—who later would do time for violating the Mann Act—captured the R&B and pop charts, and the hearts of young America, with "Sweet Little Sixteen," a saccharine ditty that might have brought a gleam of inspiration to Norman Rockwell's eye.

There would be a lot of good records during the age of innocence, but they would be anomalies. There would even be some great records.

The 1963 hit "Sally, Go 'Round the Roses," recorded by the Jaynetts, remains one of the unsurpassed rock and roll records of all time. Its strange, delved but unfathomed powers are to rhythm and blues and rock and roll what the Eleusinian Mysteries are to the realm of secret-most mythology.

How this sublime and mystical record became a hit is beyond understanding, but the gods are to be thanked for the fact that it did.

The song was written by Zelma "Zel" / "Zell" Sanders (1919-1976), who was living and working as a security guard in Harlem when she became a music entrepreneur by managing the Hearts, the girl group, formed in New York in 1954, that had its first and only hit, "Lonely Nights," under Zelma, in the early spring of 1955. Zell, who then moved to the Bronx, formed her own label, J&S, in 1956. She subsequently formed the subsidiary Scatt, Dice, Zell's, Sprout, and Omega labels, and owned and operated two song-publishing companies, Zell's Music and Idea Music.

It was the singer Lezli Valentine who wrote the song's hook: *"Saddest thing in the whole wide world, see your baby with another girl."*

The song has long provoked many different interpretations, and has been perceived as all manner of things: a veiled lesbian elegy (the word of endearment "baby," as in the song's phrase "to see your baby with another girl," having no specific gender); a siren call to the forbidden; an emanation of supernatural forces. Such was the nature of the song's immanent haunting breezes.

But the truth of it, Lezli told me, was that

Zelma merely threw together half-remembered lines from half-remembered nursery rhymes, and that Lezli's hook expressed nothing more than a sense of loneliness she felt because her husband, James Valentine, was away in the service at the time.

Born Lezli Anetta Greene in Anniston, Alabama, where her mother had traveled from New York to attend a family reunion while pregnant with her, Lezli grew up in New York and made her first record, "I Want Your Love Tonite," in the fall of 1958, when she replaced Baby Washington as the lead singer of the Hearts. "If I Had Known," recorded with the Hearts in 1961, was the first song she wrote.

Throughout the most active years of her recording career, Lezli held down a full-time job in downtown Manhattan, at 270 Broadway, as a stenographer for New York State, from whom she did her best to conceal her second career. In addition, she frequently served as Zelma's assistant and secretary at the various home "offices" in the Bronx out of which Zelma conducted her businesses. Lezli recalls that though Zelma made money from her groups, songs, and records, and owned apartment buildings on Tiffany Street in the Bronx, she always seemed hard-presssed for cash and at times even borrowed from Lezli.

It has long been believed that the Jaynetts group who recorded "Sally, Go 'Round the Roses" consisted of Ethel Davis, Mary Sue Wells, and Zell's daughter, Johnnie Louise Richardson (1935-1988), who had sung both with the Hearts and Johnnie & Joe, the duo that in 1957 had recorded the rhythm-and-blues hit "Over the Mountain; Across the Sea," written by Zell and the only rock and roll hit I can think of that had a semicolon in its title (albeit not on its record labels).

Zell wrote "Sally, Go 'Round the Roses," with Lezli providing the hook, in 1963, the year Zell entered into partnership with the record-business figure Abner Spector. She had previously used the name Jaynetts for two releases on her J&S label, in 1956 and 1958, by variations of the Hearts. On the first of these, "Where Are You Tonite" coupled with "I Wanted to Be Free," the name appeared as the Jay Netts.

Zell derived the name of the J&S label from the names Johnnie and Sanders, the former being the first name of her daughter, the latter being her own current surname. It was Lezli who came up with the name Jaynetts, or Jay Netts, fusing the "J" from J&S with the "nett" from her middle name of Anetta. The name would be used again for the girl group that recorded "Sally."

Though in the past Zell had leased rights to J&S recordings to Chess ("Over the Mountain" had been one of these), this Jaynetts record was made in direct cahoots with Abner Spector, whose Tuff Records operated under the aegis of, and had behind it the full strength of distribution by, Chess. In 1961-1962, Abner had scored big with Tuff pop hits by the Corsairs that had crossed over to the rhythm-and-blues charts. The partnership was entered into by Zell and him in mid-1963, just before "Sally, Go 'Round the Roses" came to be.

Contrary to the promotional misinformation concocted by Zell and Abner, repeated by the trade publications of the day and in the liner notes, credited to Abner Spector, of the Jaynetts' sole album, *Sally, Go 'Round the Roses* of October 1963 (Tuff LP-13), and accepted in time as history—that the Jaynetts of "Sally, Go 'Round the Roses" were Ethel Davis, Mary Sue Wells, and Johnnie Louise (in some of the press material a fourth singer, Yvonne Bushnell, is also named)—the three voices that worked the haunting magic of "Sally, Go 'Round the Roses" were in fact those of Lezli Valentine, Marie Hood, and Louise Harris.

The promotional photograph of the Jaynetts, which appeared on the cover of the sheet music and in the October 12, 1963, issue of *Billboard*, was of three girls, all of them unrecognizable now to Louise, who were stated as being, in no identified order, Ethel Davis, Mary Sue Wells, and Yvonne Bushnell.

All three of the real Jaynetts—Lezli, Louise, and Marie, the three girls who actually made the hit recording of "Sally, Go 'Round the Roses"—had been, at different times, members of the Hearts, and Lezli also helped out as Zelma's assistant and secretary. Lezli and Louise had previously recorded together on the latter's "From a Cap and a Gown," which was released, coupled with "A Prisoner to You," in 1959, on Argyle, as by Enalouise and the Hearts. (Without telling Louise about it, Zell decided to graft the first name of Louise's mother, Ena, to Louise's name, in a manner that echoed the name Zell had given her own daughter, Louise's friend Johnnie Louise.)

The members of Zelma's groups were almost constantly changing, as she hired, fired, re-hired, re-fired, and found endless new singers among the young girls who lived in the projects. The Hearts went through more than twenty different singers in fifteen years. But the outright concealment of the true identities of, and the substitution of false identities for, the singers who recorded "Sally, Go 'Round the Roses" was a new and bizarre twist.

The reasoning behind this remains a matter of conjecture. It was likely to foist off the group that toured as the Jaynetts in the wake of the success of the record as the real Jaynetts group that had recorded the hit. But, aside from "Dear Abby," which was also recorded by Lezli, Louise, and Marie, it is not even known for sure if these "fake" Jaynetts or others were the girls who recorded the other nine tracks of filler material that allowed the real Jaynetts hit single to form the basis of the album. The eleventh filler track, also used as the flip-side of the hit single (Tuff 369), was the instrumental background that had been laid down before Lezli, Marie, and Louise had been called in. Some of the filler tracks— "Dear Abby," "Keep an Eye on Her," "No Love at All"—were subsequently released by Abner as Tuff singles. The first two of these were also released with their instrumental tracks as flip-sides. On the album, "Dear Abby" was listed as "a special guest star appearance" by the Hearts, but it was released as a single by the Jaynetts and was in fact the only other track on the album, and the only other Jaynetts single, by

Lezli, Louise, and Marie.

Lezli Valentine, who was not even aware of the album until many years later, dismisses it as "terrible" and feels that the title cut is debased by even being a part of it.

An earlier group of girls—Lezli says that, "to name a few," this group included Ethel Davis, named among the "fake" Jaynetts, and whose recording under the name Vernell Hill of "Long Haired Daddy," which Abner Spector was credited with writing and producing, would be released the following year by both Tuff and Roulette; Mary Wells, also named among the "fake" Jaynetts; and Ada "Crybaby" Ray, who had recorded Zelma's "I No Longer Believe in Miracles" for Zell's the previous year—had spent a long time in the studio trying to get the song down right.

But when Lezli, Louise, and Marie were called in by Zell to replace them, the mystical magic of "Sally, Go 'Round the Roses" was achieved in a matter of hours, with the girls singing over music that already had been laid down on tape. Lezli remembers that she took a personal-leave day off from her job with the State to record "Sally, 'Go Round the Roses."

All the instrumentation, except for the guitar, was done by Artie Butler, who played the drums, piano, Hammond B-3 organ, upright bass, and tambourine that are to be heard on the record. The guitarist was Al Gorgoni. Contrary to persistent rumors that Buddy Miles, who would have been fifteen at the time, was the drummer on "Sally, Go 'Round the Roses," Artie told me that: "There was no Buddy Miles present at the session. Just me. When I finished the track, I brought in Al Gorgoni to overdub the guitar."

Twenty-three-year-old Al Gorgoni had played guitar on several Number One hits that were heard that year: "Walk Like a Man" by the Four Seasons, "Our Day Will Come" by Ruby and the Romantics, "My Boyfriend's Back" by the Angels; and he would be heard the following year on Number-One hits such as "Chapel of Love" by the Dixie-Cups and "Leader of the Pack" by the Shangri-Las.

Artie and Al laid everything down at Pat Jaques's Broadway Recording Studio, Inc., in what later became known as the Ed Sullivan Theater building, at 1697 Broadway, between Fifty-third and Fifty-fourth streets, a few blocks north of the Brill Building. Jaques himself was the engineer on the recording.

This instrumental track was used, as "Sally, 'Go Round the Roses (Instrumental Background)," as both the flip-side of the single and as one of the filler tracks on the album.

The instrumental track on the single, the one over which the voices of Lezli, Louise, and Marie are to be heard, featured a different guitarist: Carl Lynch.

As Al Gorgoni says: "Now this I'm certain of. Artie played most of the instruments on Sally. I played the guitar. That was the demo.

He did another session where Carl Lynch played guitar. That was the version that was released. The demo was on the B-side."

Looking back on "Sally, Go 'Round the Roses," Al says: "That record has a sound all its own. Sometimes the magic works, and sometimes it doesn't. I think that record was mostly a result of Artie's talent."

Carl Lynch was, like Al Gorgoni, one of the great session guitarists in New York. Known mainly for his work at Atlantic Records, for whom he had recorded with Clyde McPhatter in 1958, with Ruth Brown in 1959 and 1960, and with LaVern Baker in 1960 and 1962, and for whom, after his work on the Jaynetts record, he would record with Ben E. King in 1963 and 1965, with the Coasters in 1963, with Esther Phillips in 1964, with Solomon Burke in 1965, and with Wilson Pickett in 1968. While at Atlantic, he also did some session work for Savoy, operated out of Newark by Herman Lubinsky.

"Since I made the record," Artie Butler has said of what he did in Pat Jaques's studio that summer of 1963, when he was only twenty-one, "I have heard so many strange tales about it. There was nothing wrong with the equipment in the studio. I was going for a very different sound.

"I recorded in mono one instrument at a time. Each time I added another layer I went to another tape machine. I used two Ampex 350 tape machines at seven and a half i.p.s. [inches per second]. I kept going from one machine to the other and changed the E.Q. [equalization] and the reverb—echo, as we called it back then in the Jurassic recording period—on each layer to give it the strange sound. Each time I added another layer, the sound kept getting more distant-sounding due to the tape hiss. That is why I changed the E.Q. and the reverb on each layer. It let the new layer 'speak' over the previous layer. There was not much of a song to begin with, so I felt I had to create something that would make it its own thing. I had this sound in my mind before I started."

The lead singing was done by Lezli, with Louise and Marie singing behind her. It was also

Lezli who overdubbed the ethereal vocal parts that weave through the recording.

Lezli remembers suggesting to Zell that the song "should be sung in a round fashion, calling and answering. 'Show me, Lezli,' Zell asked. So I led and overdubbed the song."

Louise agrees that it was Lezli who basically oversaw the recording of "Sally, Go 'Round the Roses."

Abner Spector was credited with producing the recording that was made that day in the summer of 1963. But as Lezli and Louise recall it, only the three girls and an engineer were present. Louise says that she never even met Abner Spector.

It should be mentioned that Lezli, while remembering their recording definitely being done at 1697 Broadway, says it was in Studio 54. But Al Gorgoni notes that Studio 54 was not at 1697 Broadway but around the corner on West 54th Street, across from Bell Sound Studios; and Artie Butler affirms: "It was not Studio 54. It was Broadway Recording Studio. She [Lezli] is confusing the two. I know for a fact that *all* of 'Sally' was done at Broadway Recording Studio."

The filler material for the Tuff album was stated also to have been recorded at Pat Jaques's Broadway Recording Studio, but like everything else on the back of that album, this statement alone does not constitute irrefutable fact.

Artie Butler says: "I can't tell you where the rest of the album was recorded because I did not work on it. Abner Spector and I did not see eye to eye on paying people for their work, so we never worked together again. It's a shame because I do believe that the Jaynetts' career suffered because of his way of doing business. They never had a hit again. I was young and only in the business a short time at that point, so I guess I had to learn my lesson sooner or later. I believe I could have made some great records with the girls."

Artie remembers that Abner "hated" the recording when he first played it for him. "He was really angry. He felt that I wasted his money. I disagreed with him. I played the record for Jerry Leiber and Mike Stoller. They loved it and offered to buy it and reimburse him for all of his expenses. When I went back to him and told him that Leiber and Stoller loved it, he had second thoughts about it."

Though Abner never paid Artie, "he did put 'arranged by Artie Butler' on the record. That was my very first arranging credit, so I guess I did get paid in some way. Other producers started calling me to arrange sessions for them and they wanted the same band I used on 'Sally Go 'Round the Roses.' Oh, boy, was I in trouble. It was about time that I took a few arranging lessons. The record will of course always hold a special place in my heart. It hangs on my wall where my high school diploma would be hanging, had I graduated high school."

Not only did the three girls who recorded "Sally, Go 'Round the Roses" receive no credit for their achievement. They also got none of the gelt brought in by their hit recording, either. The album liner notes credited to Abner were correct in describing the big "payoff" for the Jaynetts coming "at 'Playback Time' when, in those memorable moments, they first saw the delighted looks on the faces of the musicians and heard their sincere and hearty applause." Quite a payoff indeed, especially as there were no musicians present. Abner, the producer and label-owner who wasn't there either, may have figured that money could only demean a payoff so grand and downright otherworldly as this.

"Sally, Go 'Round the Roses" appeared as a "regional breakout" in San Francisco in the *Billboard* of August 24, 1963, and a week later entered the national charts, at Number 63. By September 28, it was the Number 2 national pop hit, second only to Bobby Vinton's insipid

"Blue Velvet," which it did not overtake. It remained at Number 2 until the week of October 12, when "Blue Velvet" fell to Number 3 and it fell to Number 5.

It also became a Number 4 R&B hit, reaching that position for the week of October 19, and gained release in the United Kingdom, on the Stateside label. It was covered in both England and France. All told, it made a small fortune, of which Lezli, Louise, and Marie saw not a pittance.

"I felt sad," Lezli says about getting no credit and no money for the record.

She remembers being called in 1976 to St. Barnabus Hospital in the Bronx as Zelma lay dying. Lezli gave Zell her last drink of water. "We had quite a talk," Lezli remembered. Zelma "asked my forgiveness," she says. It was "very moving."

The copyright history of the song is as mysterious as the song itself. The song was registered for copyright by Abner's publishing firm of Winlyn Music, Inc., on July 10, 1963, and assigned registration number EU779683.

Winlyn operated out of Room 710 at 200 West Fifty-seventh Street, at the corner of Seventh Avenue, in Manhattan. The authorized agent of the copyright claimant was the attorney

Lawrence J. Greene of that address.

The original July 10, 1963, Winlyn copyright credits Lona Stevens as the co-writer, with Zelma, of the song's words and music. Lona Stevens was the pseudonym of Abner Spector's first wife, Lona Spector. (This brings to mind songs copyrighted by Lois Music, the publishing arm of Syd Nathan's King Records of Cincinnati, most of which credited as co-writer Lois Mann, a pseudonym, after the name of an old girlfriend, used by Nathan to share in the songwriting loot.)

Zell at this time was living at 1475 College Avenue in the Bronx. Abner and Lona Spector were living at 2 Sadore Lane in Yonkers.

The original, one-page contract between Zell and Abner, dated July 1, 1963, and written as from Abner to Zell, stated that Zell represented herself to be "the sole owner of the name The Jaynetts" and stated Abner to be "now in the process of producing and recording The Jaynetts singing two songs, each solely written by me, namely, 'Dear Abby' and 'Sally, Go 'Round The Roses.'"

It was stipulated that Abner "will register you and Lona Spector as the writers of said song" with the copyright office, "but it is clearly understood and agreed between us that at the end of" a five-year period, "on and as of July 1, 1968, I may, at that time or at any time thereafter, at my sole discretion, inform and contact the U.S. Copyright Office files and any and all other concerned party's files to read and reflect that I, Abner Spector, am the sole writer of said song ('Sally, Go 'Round The Roses') and, as such, am and shall be entitled, immediately and directly, to any and all writer earnings and benefits that may earn and/or accrue thereafter beginning, and as of, July 1, 1968."

Abner gained authorship rights to the song. In January of 1987 he transferred the rights from Winlyn Music, his B.M.I. firm, to Cherish Music, his ASCAP firm. In December of 1989, the master of the recording was assigned to Original Sound Record Co., Inc.; the copyright was assigned to Bonnyview Music, a Hollywood-based ASCAP firm. (The songs to which Zelma retained the rights, through her Zell's Music and Idea Music catalogues, were acquired from her grandchildren in July 1995 by Robert "Buddy" Resnik, whose Resnik Music Group of Palm Harbor, Florida, has worked with Ace Records of London in the admirable Ace reissues of many of the original recordings of those songs.) Looking at a 2008 anthology, *The Very Best of the Jaynetts*, one sees that Abner Spector is credited as the sole author of "Sally, Go 'Round the Roses."

Abner retired to Florida. He died there, on September 3, 2010, aged ninety-two. His obituary in *The Miami Herald* stated him to have been the author of "Sally, Go 'Round the Roses."

Louise Harris was born in Harlem on October 16, 1939. Though married now for many years to Donald Gatling, a former member of the Jesters vocal group, she took and kept the name of the first of her three husbands, Perry Murray, whom she married in 1958.

As Louise Harris, she made her first record, "Lonely Nights," with the Hearts (it was also their first record, and their only hit), for Baton, in early 1955, when she was just fourteen. As Louise Murray, she made her last record, "The Love I Give," for Verve, in the fall of 1965.

Sol Rabinowitz, the New York entrepreneur who ran Baton, was a friend of Alan Freed's; and he acknowledged the help of Freed, who had recently moved from WJW in Cleveland to WINS in New York, in making "Lonely Nights" a hit.

It was for Rabinowitz and Baton, in January 1957, that Ann Cole, who was born in Newark as Cynthia Coleman in 1934 and who died there in 1986, recorded what is said to have been the original version of "Got My Mo-Jo Working," which Muddy Waters is said to have picked up from her and claimed to have written.

But back to the easy-to-follow stories of Louise and Zelma and the Hearts and the Jaynetts.

Louise also told me that she was only thirteen years old when she first came to know Zelma Sanders, who was not known by that name back then. To Louise she was Miss Hicks. To others she was Zell Hicks. No one called her Zelma. Then, no marriage involved—she never married anybody—she just up and became Zelma Sanders.

And she also told me that Zell and Abner were two of a kind.

Lezli, the godmother of Zelma's granddaughter, Johnnie Louise's daughter Robin, agrees. "Zelma and Abner were about the same," she says. Zelma was bad news when it came to doing right and sharing the scratch. Though she has been somewhat mythologized into a pioneering figure, a black woman asserting herself in a white-dominated industry, she seems to have had more in common with the marauders who ran the racket than we might be led to believe by the portrait that the romance of history has painted of her.

Zelma wrote a couple more Sally songs. Her eerie "Rise Sally Rise Come to Me," copyrighted the following summer, on July 31, 1964, was recorded, for Zell's, as "Rise Sally, Come On to

Me," by Jimmy Armstrong and the Pins. The girl-group background vocals by the Pins on this intriguing but poorly recorded invocation of the dead repeated the phrases *"Sally, go 'round the roses"* (the first thing heard following the bluesy electric-guitar introduction), *"Pocketful of roses,"* and *"Rise, Sally, rise."* In that same year Zelma also had another Jaynetts group try their luck with a different flower on J&S: "Cry Behind the Daisies." And in 1968 there was "Sally Goes Up the Ladder," written by Jerry Freeman and former Majestics singer John Mitchell, but published by Zelma's company Idea Music and recorded by Freeman and Mitchell, as the Freeman Brothers, for the Sprout label, which was owned and operated by Zelma and her daughter, and which released it as "Sally Go's Up the Ladder" by the Freeman Bros.

"Sally, Go 'Round the Roses" was covered (1963) in England by Lyn Cornell and in France, as "Rose (parmi les Rose)," by both Richard Anthony and Nana Mouskouri. Many other versions of the song were later recorded: by Grace Slick, in 1966; by the Inner Circle, in 1967; by Mitch Ryder and the Detroit Wheels, in 1967; by the Australian singer Doug Parkinson and the Questions, in 1967; by Grace Markay (who went on to become a "contemporary Christian" singer), in 1968; by the Ikettes, in 1969; by the Pentangle, in 1969; by Donna Summer, as Donna Gaines, in 1971; by La Clave, in 1972; by Adam Taylor, in 1973; by Asha Puthli (the classically trained Indian singer who sang with Ornette Coleman on his 1971 *Science Fiction* album), in 1974; by Yvonne Elliman, in 1978; by the Del-Byzanteens, in 1982; by Alannah Myles, in 1995; by Question Mark and the Mysterians, in 1998; by the Damnations TX, in 1999; by Caroleen Beatty, in 2002; by Judy Collins, in 2005; by Holly Golightly, in 2005; by Algerian-born Étienne Daho with the Comateens, in 2007; by Anny Celsi, in 2009; and by Peg Simone, in 2011.

That autumn of "Sally, Go 'Round the Roses" was a strange one.

If the date of November 22, 1963, is remembered, it is usually remembered as the day that John F. Kennedy (1917-1963), whose criminal pedigree was perhaps more impressive than that of any other American president, met his end in Dallas and not as the date of the Dick Clark Show Caravan of Stars concert at the Dallas Memorial Auditorium. And yet Lee Harvey Oswald (1939-1963), the young man said to have shot the president, purchased a ticket that very morning to this rock and roll event, and only his arrest for murder presented him from attending the show that evening. He in turn was murdered two days later by Jack Ruby (1911-1967).

This convergence of Oswald and Ruby remains one of the little known and less discussed moments in rock and roll.

Ruby was a shadowland character who owned several local strip joints. He was also something of a music-business entrepreneur. One of his joints, the Vegas Club, featured an all-black five-piece band led by the Dallas musician Joseph Weldon Johnson, Jr. (1926-1991), who was better known as simply Joe Johnson. According to Johnson, his band provided a "variety of music" for Ruby's club: "progressive jazz, rock and roll, and ballads."

These quotations from Johnson are taken from the transcript of his testimony, on July 24, 1964, in the office of the United States attorney in Dallas, before a member of the general counsel's staff of the President's Commission on the Assassination of President Kennedy. None of Johnson's testimony would appear in the published *Report of the Warren Commission* that followed.

Johnson testified that he had worked for Ruby from 1956 or 1957 through the month of the assassination. He placed the date that he and Ruby parted ways as November 2, 1963, twenty days before the killing of Kennedy and twenty-two days before Ruby's murder of Oswald, the alleged assassin. Johnson said that he left because he "just wanted to change" and had been offered a job at another joint, the Castaway Club. He said that the rest of his band, except the piano-player, Leonard Wood, left Ruby's club for the Castaway with him. He did not say that the Castaway Club was run by another local mob figure, Tony Catarine, who was an acquaintance of Ruby's. According to the testimony of another band member, Walter C. Brown, the band's departure came after a "disagreement" between Johnson and Ruby.

Local legend had it that Ruby harbored a dislike of musicians that dated to the first club, the Silver Spur, that he ran in Dallas, back in 1951. During a brawl that year at the Silver Spur, the Dallas rockabilly guitarist Willis "Dub" Dickerson (1927-1979) bit off the tip of Ruby's left forefinger. As Diana Hunter and Alice Anderson put it in their book, *Jack Ruby's Girls* (1970): "From that time on, Ruby had a heat on against musicians."

Joe Johnson was asked: "Did Jack Ruby attempt to promote any records for you?"

The reply was: "He had talked about it. He never did promote any records for me."

A contract dated May 19, 1959, between Joe Johnson and Cascade Records of Los Angeles named Jack Ruby, who approved the contract, as the "agent for" Johnson. An addendum to this contract, dated three days later, is also signed by Al Kavelin of Cascade Records and Joe Johnson, and approved by the signature of "Jack Ruby, Agent for Joe W. Johnson."

May 1959 was when radio station KROW in Oakland was taken over by McLendon Broadcasting, which was operated out of Dallas by Gordon McLendon (1921-1986). The station became KABL. *The San Mateo Times* of Monday, May 11, 1959, reported that the station in neighboring Oakland "sure did sound like it was going crazy" over the previous three days of weekend broadcasting. "The programming was not unlike the usual 'rock and roll' stations around the area, with one major exception." This was: "Each song announced turned out to be a thing called 'Gila Monster.'" The reporter, Bob Foster, declared: "It is pretty obvious that the new management of the station is using this method to get attention for its wild and wooly operation." As for "Gila Monster" itself: "the tune is such a horrid thing."

"Gila Monster," on the Cascade label, was by Joe Johnson. And it got there because of Jack Ruby.

Cascade Records, Inc., had filed as a business on March 4, 1959, two months before McLendon Broadcasting of Dallas inaugurated its new Oakland station by broadcasting "Gila Monster" for three days running. On the record label, Ed Carrell is credited as the sole songwriter of "Gila Monster," but a search of the B.M.I. archives shows McLendon to be named as the song's co-writer. Furthermore, Gordon McLendon was the executive producer of *The Giant Gila Monster*, the low-budget picture, released in June 1959, that the "Gila Monster" record was concocted to tie into.

Al Kavelin would go on some months later, in early 1960, to found Lute Records, which had one of the biggest hits of that year with the novelty record "Alley-Oop" by the Hollywood Argyles. It appeared on the charts in May 1960, a year to the month after the misadventures of "Gila Monster."

In its June 15, 1959, review of "Gila Monster," *Billboard* dismissed it as a "novelty blues" whose lyric "describes the Gila monster, looking like he wants to do the rock and roll." But there are those who today treasure this record as one of the artefacts of rock and roll at its trashiest depths.

Somehow this all brings to mind Homer Henderson's great record of 1985, "Lee Harvey Was a Friend of Mine."

Yes, that autumn of "Sally, Go 'Round the Roses" was a strange one.

The Beatles, sort of a silly girl group with male genitals, who came along a few months after Sally came and went around the roses, were mere pap. It would not be until nearly two years after "Sally, Go 'Round the Roses"—the summer of 1965, which began with the blast of the Rolling Stones' "Satisfaction" and culminated with the further blast of Bob Dylan's *Highway 61 Revisited*—that resurrection would truly come, in a sudden exundant thundering wave.

FOUR

George Goldner was in his early thirties, married to a Latin-American woman, and an aficionado of the recent mambo craze when he started his Tico recording company in 1948. Tico became the dominant label in Latin music, and less than two years after its founding, Goldner began a subsidiary label, Rama, to take advantage of the new black doo-wop music. With the immense success of Rama's recording of the Crows' "Gee," Goldner started Gee Records in 1954. It was Goldner who subsequently "discovered" Frankie Lymon and the Teenagers, whose first and biggest hit, "Why Do Fools Fall in Love," was released by Gee in early 1956.

"George Goldner," as one old-timer told me, "was the genius of the business."

We are still sitting around a big table in the back room of a restaurant—much talk of recent surgeries and present medical woes; much ordering of eggs and sausages to be prepared in exacting and arcane Italianate manners—and as this is said, and while others concur, Hy Weiss, another old-timer from that wide-open age of the masque of innocence, scowls benignly, nonchalantly shakes his head, and points silently, almost privately, to himself.

"Don't mention George Goldner," says Weiss (just some coffee, plain eggs, no sausage). "He was a figment of my imagination." This dismissal is his way of saying that it was he, not Goldner, who found Frankie Lymon: "I gave him the Teenagers."

Whether or not Goldner was the genius maximus of the business, one thing was certain: by the fall of 1955, Goldner had cut in a new partner, Joe Kolsky, the brother of a man named Phil Kahl, who was in partnership in music-publishing with one Moishe Levy.

It is difficult to state with certainty the roles played by the brothers Kahl and Kolsky in what became Goldner's dance in the dark with Moishe Levy. Kahl, who had been a manager of Disney Music, had entered into open alliance with Levy in early 1953, with the formation of Patricia Music, a publishing operation that also handled several performers, including the brilliant but doomed and demon-beset jazz pianist Bud Powell. Whatever his experience in the music business, Kahl was known as Fingers—a reference, not so much sinister as cynical, to his primary career as a hairdresser at the Concord Hotel in the Catskills. Kolsky, presented in the course of business as a produce tycoon, was in fact the proprietor of a fruit stand in the Bronx.

The Bronx. It was where Hy Weiss lived. It was where Phil Spector was born. It was where Dion, the greatest of the white doo-wop masters, came from. Dion had a group called the Timberlanes, then he had the Belmonts.

"A friend of mine sent them to me," remembers Wassel, who helped get them a deal.

"Who was your friend?"

"Some guy."

"Just some guy?"

"A wiseguy."

Wassel says the guy is still alive, says he'll call to ask if it's all right for me to use his name.

Like Frankie Lymon and the Teenagers, another Bronx group, whose cute, coy "Why Do Fools Fall in Love" belied the heroin-ridden fate of thirteen-year-old Lymon, who would die unknown of an overdose at twenty-five, Dion was another junkie who played his part in the masque of innocence. It would not be until 1961, after the Belmonts, with hits such as "Runaround Sue" and "The Wanderer," that Dion's sound got tough. His first Top Ten hit, with the Belmonts, in 1959, cute and coy, was "A Teenager in Love," a record that, like Lymon's fare, betrayed no hint of either track-marks or worldliness.

And the Bronx was where Moishe Levy grew up. He went by the name of Morris, but those who knew him called him Moe when they didn't call him Moishe. He was in his early twenties when he took over Birdland, the celebrated jazz nightclub, named for Charlie "Bird" Parker, that opened in 1949 on Fifty-second Street at Broadway. Even then there was a mythology about the man who called himself Morris Levy. He had won control of the joint in a card game, it was said—drawing three sevens, playing one on one against the owner—though many swear that Levy never gambled except for an occasional game of craps. He had started out as a kid flipping hamburgers at the Turf, which, like Jack Dempsey's, faced Broadway from the street level of the Brill Building. He had then become a photo developer of pictures taken of patrons by nightclub camera girls. Then he operated coatcheck concessions in clubs throughout town. Then, mysteriously, he owned clubs: not only

Birdland and its sister club, Birdland of Miami, but the Royal Roost, Bop City, the Downbeat, the Embers, and the Round Table were all, at one time or another, said, known, or rumored to have been Levy's joints.

Then there was this business with the hairdresser and the fruit-vendor. Levy came to Hy Weiss one day, told him that he wanted to buy into Hy's record company. Levy ended up with a piece of Maureen Music, the publishing adjunct of Old Town, named for Hy's daughter. Meanwhile, George Goldner was on a roll in 1955 and was just about to come forth with Frankie Lymon and the Teenagers. George may have been the genius of the business, but he was not without the Achilles' heel that had brought down the multitude of his lessers. He was a degenerate gambler. By 1957, Goldner's record companies, already given over to Levy's forces, were subsumed by a new company, Roulette, whose partners were stated to be Goldner and Kolsky, and whose president was stated to be Levy. Within three months, Goldner was out of the picture altogether, his interest in Roulette, as well as all participation in the rights to his Tico, Rama, and Gee catalogues, ceded wholly to what *Billboard* referred to as "the Morris Levy combine."

Roulette under Levy prospered well into the

sixties. "Peppermint Twist" by Joey Dee—Joey DiNicola of Passaic, New Jersey—released by Roulette in late 1961, was a bigger hit than Chubby Checker's version of "The Twist," and made the Peppermint Lounge, believed to be another Levy property, the most celebrated nightclub in America. It was on Roulette, too, that Arkansas-born Ronnie Hawkins had his first Top 40 hit, "Mary Lou" in 1959. Hawkins remained with Levy and Roulette through 1963, two years before members of his band, the Hawks, began working with Bob Dylan.

For all the wealth it brought him, Morris Levy never much cared for rock and roll, a friend of his told me. "Morris loved jazz. He didn't like rock and roll."

George Goldner went on to have some success with two new companies, End and Gone, but these labels, too, ended up in Levy's hands. With the songwriting team of Leiber and Stoller, he went on, in 1964, to form yet another company, Red Bird, which had its share of hits, by the Shangri-Las and others; but both the partnership and the label soon dissolved, and Goldner died a few years later, in 1970, at the age of fifty-two.

Not only was he a genius, says one who knew him, in way of epitaph, but "he was one hell of a sharp dresser, too."

But what of Morris Levy's genius? In a group, as at that big round back-room table, the old-timers are wary, evasive in answering.

"He could spot a winner," says one.

"The 'essence of his genius'?" smiles another, wryly using the phrase I had offered. "Robbing everybody."

"He never gambled."

"He took over underdogs."

"Morris hated to give up money. Money was his god, and he was devout in his religion."

"What was that I was saying? 'This is my grocery store. I do all the robbin' here.'"

"If you sold a million records, he'd say you sold a hundred thousand. Moe was pretty sharp with that. That was his thing."

"But he wasn't doing anything that everybody else wasn't doing."

"All thieves."

"Not thieves," objects Hy Weiss. "They just did business their own way. It was a way of business."

"People say how they got robbed," says Hy Weiss. "They didn't get robbed. I didn't rob anybody and neither did a lot of other people that are accused. Why? Because at that particular time, everybody was offering what they had for sale. In fact, I had a song called 'So Fine'"— a minor Old Town hit by the Fiestas, a Newark group, in 1959—"and I gave it up. Somebody said they owned it, I says good-bye like an idiot. That wouldn't happen again in a million years, you know what I'm saying?"

FIVE

One of my favorite Hy Weiss stories was told to me by Billy Miller of Norton Records. It was early August 1992:

"I get this call," says Billy, "at eight in the morning and this guy's screaming at me."

"'You're fuckin' with my masters.'

"'Huh? What? Who is this?'

"'Hy Weiss. Old Town Records. You're fuckin' with my masters.'

"He told me that we had put 'Big Mary's House' by the Solitaires on one of our albums. I pointed out that this wasn't the case, but he just kept going:

"'Don't give me that, I've heard all of this shit before. You're fuckin' with my masters.'

"'Mr. Weiss, I can look into it, but I'm positive we never released anything by the Solitaires or anything that was on Old Town.'

"'Yeah, yeah, right. You don't know who you're fuckin' with.'

"'I can look into it, but…'

"'You do that. I'm gonna call you back at four o'clock and I want some answers.'

"I was telling him the truth, I realized that he was not talking about something Norton had released, but instead it was an album on another label that we only had a few copies of that we had purchased from a distributor.

"Shortly after Hy Weiss's call, we received word that Miriam's father had died that morning. I had family matters to attend to, so I didn't look into where I'd gotten the album with the Solitaires from. Four o'clock sharp, the phone rings.

"'Well?' Hy Weiss. Still mad as hell.

"'I'm sorry, Mr. Weiss. I can tell you this album with your track was something on another label that wasn't ours.'

'Whose is it?'

"'Mr. Weiss, again I'm sorry. I haven't had a chance to track down any information. We had a death in the family since you called. My father-in-law passed away.'

"Suddenly he did a complete about-face and became the sweetest guy in the world.

"'Oh, my. How old was he? Had he been ill?'

"I told him no, it was sudden, outside his apartment in Florida. Illness, death, and Florida. I hit on something bigger than the Solitaires. Hy was now speaking calmly and he was very concerned. He wanted to know if my wife was O.K. 'Please pass along my condolences to the family.' And then he closed with, 'Look, you seem like a nice kid. Let me tell you, records like these tend to have babies. So from now on, just be careful who you deal with.'"

SIX

The most important figure in the introduction of rock and roll—real rock and roll—to white America was the legendary Alan Freed (1922-65), who began broadcasting R&B records over WJW in Cleveland in the summer of 1951. Though the audience for the records he played was predominantly black, his Judaeo-Christian benediction of the music served to draw an increasingly integrated group of listeners. By 1953 his rock and roll touring shows, which featured the likes of Count Basie and Lester Young as well as of Big Joe Turner, Wynonie Harris, Ruth Brown, and the Clovers, were a success and a sensation, bringing him controversial celebrity and fortune both. When he moved to New York to work at WINS in the late summer of 1954—the cusp of rock and roll's golden and silver ages, he came as the most powerful disc jockey in the land.

The man who took control of his career in New York was Morris Levy.

"That was the secret of Moishe's success," I was told. "He controlled Freed." And, in those pay-for-play days, Freed, whose plays were the biggest, got the biggest pay. "Every record company that was in business selling R&B had a deal with Alan Freed. Atlantic, King, Federal, all of them. And they all had to come up with the money. That's the way it was. Freed made money. Morris made money."

In a group, these are the things that are said, and in all of what is said there is truth. These men know what they are talking about, and there seems to be no special fondness for Levy among them.

There are a lot of stories from the Birdland days. It was Irving Levy, Moishe's brother, that managed the joint.

"He was a sweetheart, Irving. I was there the night he was killed. He had a hooker there, didn't want her there, and he chased her out. Her husband caused a big commotion, stabbed Irving, killed him. So then it was like open season. All the jukebox guys used to hang in the Birdland mostly. And everybody's out for the husband. You never seen more people getting shot left and right, everybody thinking they've got the guy."

"He loved broads," one says of Morris, who would marry and divorce several times.

But what of all the tales of Levy's being deeper into the Mob than the rest of them?

"Bullshit."

But alone, some speak differently. One takes me aside, his arm around me, whispering though we are in earshot of no one.

"Let me tell you," he says. His hushed words are delivered slowly and surely: "Morris simply could not have done what he did alone."

It became known late in 1956 that the House Subcommittee on Legislative Oversight was preparing to investigate commercial bribery in the music industry. A few months later it was reported, "The multi-faceted business relationship between deejay-impresario Alan Freed and manager-publisher Morris Levy was severed abruptly altho amicably last week by consent of the parties involved."

Alan Freed, broken by the ensuing scandals of the lengthy payola hearings, died impoverished and disgraced in the year that later brought the sudden exundant wave of rock and roll's resurrection. As for Levy, he was charged in 1986 on counts of criminal collusion and conspiracy with several alleged mafiosi, and was convicted in 1988. Following the failure of an appeal, he was scheduled to report to federal prison when, in the spring of 1990, age sixty-two, he died at the manor house of his estate, a thirteen hundred acre horse farm in Ghent, New York.

SEVEN

Of course, the payola scandals stopped nothing. Alan Freed was just the sacrificial fatted calf. Juggy Gayles (1913-2000), the legendary song-plugger—the man who broke "White Christmas" for Irving Berlin, the man who got Kate Smith to take up Berlin's "God Bless America"—had known Freed since the disc jockey's early days in Cleveland. "What can I tell ya?" Gayles said when I asked him about Freed and payola. Freed, he said, "was a genius, and he was a power to reckon with." But, at the same time, "Freed was a schmuck. He went around and shot his mouth off. They would've forgot about him if he had kept his mouth shut." As Gayles implied, rock and roll and payola were inseparable. It went back to the big-band days. "Some of those Mickey Mouse bandleaders, we'd slip 'em ten bucks to play a chorus because we needed a quick plug," said Juggy. But with the rise of rock and roll, "Payola was all over the place. Booze, bribes, and broads: that was rock and roll."

Inquisition, prosecution mattered not. At the masque of innocence, it was business as usual.

"There was nothing wrong with it," says Hy Weiss. "What was that guy, the disc jockey from Boston who became head of Warner Brothers Records? Joe Smith, that's him. Well, what did he say about me? He said I made up the fifty-dollar handshake."

Joe Smith would later have his own tales to tell, such as the ordeal of signing Van Morrison, who was under contract to dark forces:

"He was the artist that I had coveted, but I didn't know where to find him and I didn't know who had his contract. I called Joe Scandore, who was Don Rickles's manager. The mob guys called him the *elegante* of Brooklyn. And Joe knew about people. I said, 'Joe, find out what I got to do to get his contract.'

"We found him. He was in a basement in Cambridge with the immigration people trying to throw him out, and there was no record label, and he was broke. Scandore found out that they'd sell the contract; they wanted twenty thousand dollars for the contract. So I had to meet a guy at six o'clock at night on the third floor of a warehouse on Tenth Avenue in Manhattan. The guy said to bring the money. I wasn't feeling very good about that. I had the cab wait and I walk up the stairs and I knock on the door and I come in and it's central casting. There's a big wide guy sitting behind the desk and a big tall guy standing beside him. I come in and I say, 'I'm Joe Smith, I'm with Warners, I need to talk.' I talk to somebody. He says, 'You got the money?' I say, 'Yes, you got the contract?' 'Let's have the money.' 'The contract, is it signed?' 'It's signed.' 'Are you authorized to sign it?' 'What?' 'Okay, okay.' Now what I'm concerned about is, I'm gonna take the contract, go outside, and something's going to hit me in the side of the head, and the next thing I won't have a contract. I jump from the third floor landing to the second floor, I almost broke my foot, and I ran out onto the street and got into the cab and went back and put the contract in the safe at the Warner office."

This was how Van Morrison's first hit album, *Moondance*, came to be recorded, for Warner Bros., in 1969.

But back to Hy Weiss and his fifty-dollar handshakes, which in time attracted the attention of the Feds.

"One day the door opened and Internal Revenue walked in. I said, 'Yes?' They said, 'Well, we understand you're doing business with disc jockeys,' and so on. I said, 'What's wrong with that? Everybody's doing business with disc jockeys.' He said, 'But you gave somebody five thousand dollars.' And I said, 'Who was that, pray tell?' He said, 'You gave it to Alan Freed.' I said, 'I *gave* it to him?' He says, 'Yeah.' I said, 'Well, wait awhile, let me look at something.' I picked out a check and showed it to him with a little note. He said, 'What's that?' I said, 'It was a *loooaan*.' He laughed.

"That night we went out to the track, out to dinner, me and the guy from the I.R.S. I had to sit there and give him winners.

"I could tell you the end of the story," Weiss concludes, "but I can't get a friend of mine in trouble."

That reminds someone of another investigating agent. "This agent, he sounds all serious: 'I want to talk to you.' Then he holds up this little hand-lettered sign: I'M WIRED."

EIGHT

Bookies, Broadway, the Brill Building, the Boys.

My buddy Gene Sculatti, a true connoisseur of the bizarries that lurk beneath the stones of popular culture's forgotten back streets, went off in search of a guy named Tony Bruno, a singer who in 1967 released an album called The *Beauty of Bruno*, an artefact equal in rarity and obscurity to *Little Joe Sure Can Sing*, the album, released a year later, that Joe Pesci recorded under the name of Little Joe Ritchie. Both these young men were from New Jersey.

Those were strange days, as Jim Morrison sang in the year of *The Beauty of Bruno*. People remember "Strange Days," as well they should. But what of Hank Ballard's reappearance on the R&B charts in 1968—Hank Ballard, who had been at it since 1952, had shotgun-blasted the sensibilities of America in 1954 with "Work with Me, Annie" and "Sexy Ways," had originated "The Twist" in 1959, and was still only thirty-two when he came back with "How You Gonna Get Respect (When You Haven't Cut Your Process Yet)"? Well, as Jim Morrison had said it, and truly enough: people are strange.

My buddy Gene finally found Tony Bruno, who was living quietly in Florida. Bruno generously shared with him the story of how he got into the music business, back in 1960:

"I was hangin' around the Brill Building, takin' action for this bookie from New Jersey. I was doing pretty well, so he set me up with an office, and we pretended it was a record label. I had my desk, a small turntable, and eight or nine phones."

The lettering on the office door read NOMAR RECORDS, the nonce word Nomar being a partial reverse spelling of the surname of Bruno's boss. It was inevitable, in that hive of aspiration and hustling that was the Brill Building, that someone should eventually knock on the door of Nomar Records looking for a deal. That inevitability came in the form of Maxine Brown, a young singer from South Carolina bearing an acetate demonstration recording of a song she'd written called "All in My Mind." To press and release the record would lend the front a further illusory air of legitimacy.

But something went wrong. Maxine Brown's "All in My Mind," released by Nomar Records in December of 1960, entered the R&B charts during the following month and eventually became one of the major hits of the year, rising to Number 2 on the R&B charts, crossing over to the pop Top Twenty, and selling about eight hundred thousand copies before it ran its course. Another Maxine Brown hit, almost as big, followed. By comparison, the bookmaking operation, eight phones and all, seemed little more than a chump-change racket. It was thus that Tony Bruno became a producer and songwriter, and, after years of prospering as such, gave unto the world *The Beauty of Bruno*.

NINE

Jesse Stone (1901-1999)—patriarch of rock and roll, conjurer in 1949 of the classic rock and roll bass-pattern that defined the soul of R&B, author in 1954 of "Shake, Rattle, and Roll," the Homeric bellows of the crown of rock and roll's golden age—told me about the time he tried to retire:

"I moved out to California to take it easy, I laid on the beach listening to ball games for about a year. Some guy came looking for me one day, told me that he was snowed under with the Twist craze, asked me if I could help him out with a few arrangements.

"I didn't know it then, but that was the end of my retirement. Before I knew it, I was doing stuff for all sorts of Hollywood people. I ended up at Frank Sinatra's new company, Reprise.

"A bunch of gangsters from Chicago offered

me a job running a record company there. I turned them down. They made me another offer. I turned them down again. They kept raising the price. Eventually it was too good to refuse. So I moved to Chicago.

"These guys weren't interested in recording. They just wanted a front. They had the top floor of the Playboy Building. They fixed me up in the most lavish, elaborate office that I had ever seen. I said, 'I don't need all this room.' 'Don't worry about it.' They would come in and hang around in the morning, overseeing all the booking action that was being done on the telephones. Then, after lunch, at one o'clock, the place turned into a recording company. It was Roy Love, Huddie, and those guys. Huddie at that time was the big boss of the whole North Side. The record company, Ran-Dee Records, was named after his grandkid.

"It was a mess. These guys were bringin' in whatever chicks they were involved with, Playboy bunnies, whatever, to make records. They would just feed these chicks some line and send 'em to me. None of them could sing.

"One day I said, 'The reason the records ain't selling is we're not getting any publicity. I need to send out some press releases.' They said, 'O.K., we'll get you a printin' press.' I figured they'd get me one of those little things you set on a table and turn the handle. No. They got me a thirty-thousand-dollar A.B. Dick multicolor lithograph press. It came to the building on a big truck. 'I don't know how to work this thing.' 'Don't worry about it.' It was crazy.

"They were giving me plenty of money. *Plenty* of money. But I became frightened. They blew some guy away on the East Side, some guy they'd put in as alderman or something, and he'd double-crossed them. And they'd have business meetings in my office, and I'd hear them talking: 'Did you see the expression on that guy's face when I told him that this was his last day?' This is what I would hear. They'd be talkin' about it like they were discussin' a poker game: 'He's lookin' in the muzzle and his eyes are gettin' bigger and bigger, and I blow him away.' That sort of thing was getting to me. I figured, uh-oh, I gotta get out of here.

"I slowly turned the operation over to Huddie's son, Lenny Loveman. He'd been thrown out of a bunch of colleges, and they didn't know what to do with him. I put him in charge of the record company. They were really appreciative. They gave me twenty-four thousand dollars, and I cut out of there. I told them I was going back to New York, but I really went to Englewood, New

Jersey. I thought they might come looking for me. One day I got a call at Roosevelt Music. Guy on the line said, 'Anything you ever need, we'll be right here."

TEN

Jubilee Records, founded in Washington, DC in 1946 by Herb Abramson, and taken over by Jerry Blaine in 1947, epitomized the scattershot approach of the mongrel labels: record, buy, or lease anything you could, get it out there, and see what shook. Jubilee put out records by the Delta Rhythm Boys, Charlie Mingus, Enzo Stuarti, the Orioles, and a slew of characters who specialized in risqué "party" records. The rarest of all rock and roll records, the example of scattershot negligence *par excellence*, was released, nominally, by Jubilee in 1952: "Stormy Weather" by the Five Sharps, of which only one unbroken, 78-rpm copy is known to exist, is now valued at more than fifty grand.

Jerry Blaine also operated various Jubilee subsidiary labels: Josie brought forth the Cadillacs and their hit "Speedoo"; Gross was reserved for albums by Doug Clark and the Hot Nuts. In early 1962 he started to distribute some releases on Willie "Tony" Ewing's little Chex label.

It was in June of that year that young Freddy DeMann of Brooklyn began working for Blaine as a promotion man of the non-defenestrating kind. The exact date was June 5, Freddy's twenty-third birthday.

DeMann, who twenty-one years later became Madonna's manager, remembers Blaine as a gruff-speaking man given to talk of lavish excess. He was at the Jubilee office when somebody came in looking to sell a recording to Blaine.

"Whadaya want for it?" Blaine demanded.

A price of five hundred dollars was suggested with some hesitation.

"Five hundred?" growled Blaine. "Shit, man, I pay more than that for whores."

Blaine, however, gave DeMann nothing in the way of pay-for-play gelt when he sent him out in early 1962 to promote "I Love You" by the Volumes on Chex. Without the cash, DeMann discovered, the record was trash: it had entered the pop charts but was in limbo.

Freddy met a fellow promotion man, a guy named Danny Driscoll who worked for Smash, a subsidiary of Mercury. Danny tried to shore him.

"He was a big fat guy," DeMann says. "Jovial. Funny. 'Call me Fat Ass,' he used to say. 'I'm not gonna call you Fat Ass,' I said. 'Come on, everybody calls me Fat Ass.' He was a colorful guy. Then one day they found him dead in a car. He was a fag, and the story I heard is that some sailor killed him or something like that. But I don't know if that's the truth. Maybe the Boys got him. I have no clue."

That was one thing that Freddy learned quickly: it was a strange racket. The Boys cast a lot of shadows, there were a lot of maybes as to what went on. Like many of the promotion guys in the early sixties, he hung out at Al & Dick's, a joint on Fifty-fourth Street near Broadway that went back to the Volstead Act days, when the entertainer Texas Guinan, the darling of the underworld, ran it and many other Broadway boîtes de nuit in cahoots with the Boys of that time. Texas Guinan, a role model and inspiration for Mae West, was remembered for her greeting to patrons: "Hello, suckers." But another remark attributed to her held its wisdom as the old days on Broadway gave way to the new: "Success has killed more men than bullets."

DeMann describes the clientele of Al & Dick's as "a Runyonesque group of people. They were all guys in suits with slick black hair. Pompadours, that kind of thing." The disc jockeys, the industry guys, the artists, the friends of friends.

"We all looked alike. It was an exciting world to come into. And I was, believe me, brand new. And, yes, I knew there were guys there that could get the job done."

In the end, without any cash to slip into the sleeves of "I Love You," Freddy, after a long roundabout journey among unresponsive disc jockeys, found himself in Philadelphia. It was there, in the studio office of Jerry Blavat, that he laid down his lantern.

"So, anyway," Blavat says, "I'm doing the radio show, and the promotion men come to see me. I get a knock at the door, and I say to Kilocycle Pete, 'Answer the door,' which he normally does.

"So it's this young guy. His name is Freddy DeMann. He says, 'I got a record I want you to listen to, and I've got a problem.' I said, 'What's the problem?' He says, 'Nobody will play this record. You're my last resort. I'm gonna lose my gig.' He says, 'There's no money on this record. I have no money for the record.' I said, 'Freddy, let me tell you something. Number one, I don't take money. If I like the record, I play it. My mother can come to me with a record and say, "Your uncle made this record." If I don't like the record, I'm not gonna play it. Because for my teenagers, for my audience, I have in my mind the sound I'm gonna present.' To make a long story short, he sits with me while I do the radio show. I listen to the record. I flip over the record. Nobody wants to play the record because they're all looking for this"—he rubs his thumb and two fingers in the universal baksheesh gesture—"and he doesn't have it. I play the record, bust the record wide open. From that moment on, Freddy DeMann and I became friends. His boss, Jerry Blaine, wanted to know, 'How did you get the Geator to play this record with no money?'" (That's Blavat, see, the Geator with the Heater, etymology approximately as such: the nickname Geator back-formed from the nickname Gater to rhyme with heater, as in let's-get-down-with-the-sound-and-turn-that-car-heater-up-on-this-cold-Philly-night.) "And Freddy explained to him, 'He liked the record, man, he liked the record.' And that's the way I was from the very beginning to now. You could be my best buddy, but if I don't like the record, I'm not gonna play it."

Blavat was twenty-two years old and making over a hundred grand a year.

"I mean, back in 1962, that's a lot of money for a little cockroach kid from South Philadelphia."

ELEVEN

The ultimate source for *C'era una volta in America*, Sergio Leone's 1984 movie about the Jewish Mob in New York in the early part of the twentieth century, was a 1952 book by Harry Gray, *The Hoods*, which Robert De Niro, the picture's star, had read as a Signet paperback and long had wanted to see transmuted to a movie. In preparing for his role, De Niro wanted to meet Meyer Lansky, whose mannerisms and mien he sought to emulate in his character. Lansky, nearing eighty and living in seclusion in Miami, was a very difficult man to reach.

"We met at Rocco Maselli's jewelry store in Manhattan," Blavat says. "This guy came in and he was introduced to me, and then I was introduced to De Niro. Then the guy, De Niro's buddy, asked me if I could, you know, get him an audience with Lansky."

How did this guy know to come to you?

"Well, because he knew who I was. He may have been connected or whatever."

Jerry did what he could. Back in Philly, he asked the forces that be if such an audience could be arranged. It was Nicky Scarfo, the new boss, who returned the verdict of imperial thumbs-down to De Niro.

Blavat, who was offered a small part in the picture, ended up having hernia surgery as the American cast and crew left for filming in Italy. On the last day of 1982, Lansky himself entered a hospital, and he died there fifteen days later, while the movie known in English as *Once Upon a Time in America* was in production.

TWELVE

C'era una volta a Filadelfia...

Gerald Joseph Blavat was born, in Philly, on July 3, 1940. "See," he says, "when I was a kid growing up, there were four corners in the neighborhood. Pat's Luncheonette, the grocery store, the Tap Room, and a variety store. These were the four corners of South 17th and Mifflin streets. The younger guys hung on one corner. Across the street were the older guys. Then, in the Tap Room, were the older wiseguys. And the variety-store corner, the people in the neighborhood would come in and buy blah, blah, blah, I don't know. And up the side street, the older guys would shoot craps.

"When you grew up in that neighborhood, you knew everybody. You knew everybody. They used to call me Shorts when I was a kid because I was the smallest little guy. But I always knew and respected older people. When I was twelve I was hanging out in the social club with guys seventeen, eighteen years old. By the time I was sixteen, I was donning a black Stetson, black continental suit, going into clubs and bars. But I knew how to act, so I always acted older."

Like the Mob in America, Jerry was Jewish and Italian. His father, known as Gimpy Lou, or simply the Gimp, was with the Jewish crew. "He was in the numbers business When I was a kid, they would ship me off to a day nursery at St. Monica's at six in the morning. We lived in a row house on a street where there were only six houses—everything else was garages—and our house would turn into a bookie joint with all the top Jewish guys working it. Moishe, Sammy, Mickey. When I came home from the day nursery at five, it would turn back into a regular house."

His mother came from the same town in the Chieti province of Abruzzi as did the wife of Angelo Bruno, the Sicilian-born mafioso to whom control of Philadelphia passed from Joe Ida in the late '50s. It was thus as a boy, through his father's involvement in the rackets, more through his mother's friendship with Angelo's wife, that Jerry came to know the ascendant boss before the advent of his imperium.

"My father divorced my mother, and I was supposed to be getting support checks, which were supposed to go to my mother. It's supposed to be, like, my money, but, with the support checks, he buys me a car. This had to be '56. Yeah. It was a '56 Plymouth Fury, the one with the push-buttons and the fins.

"Well, he was going with a girl by the name of Gloria, a hat-check girl, a kid, at Palumbo's. He was in his late forties. She was maybe nineteen or twenty, Very attractive. So, I'd be playing hooky from school, and I would be fucking this girl, never knowing that this was my father's cumare. One day I hear the door open. The apartment is dark. I hear the door close. I don't know who it was. I go back to school, because I would hooky just to fuck. The next day, or the following week, or whenever, he gets in a beef and knocks her eye out: 'You're fuckin' my son,' blah, blah, blah.

"Then one day he's driving me in my car. He pulls over near where they were building the Walt Whitman Bridge, and he gets this big fat broad, puts her in the back of the car, and he says, 'Let's drive down to the lakes.' Now, I'm still sixteen; this is after the incident with the other broad. He says, 'You wanna get blown?' I said, 'I'll get blown, why not?' He says, 'O.K., go take a walk, I'm gonna get blown first.' So I go take a walk, and I come back five minutes later, and he says to this broad, 'O.K., my son.' He takes a walk and I get blown.

"That was our relationship. But with the car, what does he do to make it up to this Gloria after the puts her eye out? He gives her my car. He takes it and he says to her, 'I bought you a brand-new car.' It was my fuckin' car, from the support money. He took my Plymouth Fury. He takes the car, gives it to her, then never pays any of the payments on it after she has it. They repossess the car, and she comes after me. That was my old man."

To this day, Jerry Blavat is a churchgoing Roman Catholic.

Blavat had been one of the kids who danced on the WFIL-TV show *American Bandstand* in the days before the show's original host, Bob Horn, banished in the wake of scandals involving drunk-driving and allegations of sex with a minor, was replaced, in the summer of 1956, by Dick Clark, the cultural hygienist whose smile of cleanliness and rectitude was the smile of milk-and-cookies rock and roll. Another of the dancers from the Horn show, Danny Rapp, had helped to form and was the lead singer in a local group called the Juvenaires. In 1957 the group became Danny and the Juniors. Their first record, "At the Hop," released toward the end of that year, was one of the the biggest hits of 1958. When the group set out to tour, it was with Jerry Blavat as their road-manager and shepherd.

"These kids were innocent," Jerry says. "I used to get them laid. That was the biggest thing they wanted to do. I was a kid, eighteen, on the road. I would take them to, say, Wheeling, West Virginia. One time I went in, and I think it was ten bucks apiece to get laid. They were only making forty bucks a week. I handled all the money. So, one kid, wanted to get fucked a second time. I said, 'Look, you just got laid, you're not gonna be able to get it up.' Yeah, yeah, yeah. 'I'm in love with this fuckin' broad.' So I made a deal with the madam: 'He wants to go a second time.' She said, 'O.K., give me eight dollars.' He went back up to the room, and we're all waiting. The madam came and said, 'Look, he's gotta be outa there very shortly.' We're still waiting. The madam comes and she says, 'I'm getting him out of here.' She goes upstairs, I hear a commotion, yelling and screaming. He doesn't wanna leave until he gets a hard-on. She comes back down, she calls the cops. The cops come, and they almost pinch us because it was protected. He wants his money back, the eight bucks.

I said, 'Fuck you and your fucking money, let's get out of here.'"

Though, like all else, without meaning. the confluence is inviting: a few years ago, De Niro told me that, if memory served him, "At the Hop" may have been the first record to which he danced. I think of him dancing, Blavat meanwhile staying the cops as the errant Junior frustratedly zippers, neither of them knowing of their own futures, or the jewelry-store meeting to come. It was in the spring of 1983, not long after that meeting, that Danny Rapp, age forty-one, committed suicide.

As immensely successful as it was, "At the Hop" was pretty much the end as well as the beginning of Danny and the Juniors. When Blavat came off the road with them for the last time, in 1960, they were fading fast. Jerry, however, had just begun.

"There was this nightclub in South Philadelphia called the Venus. And, remember, this is when rock and roll is not being featured in clubs. I mean, this was a lounge where wiseguys go and drink and pick up broads and things like that. I mean, it was the Venus Lounge in South Philadelphia. So, I had just made a score coming off the road. I think I had, like, eight hundred bucks, and I started to shoot craps at 17th and Mifflin with the older guys. And Don Pinto, who owned the club, was there. Guys were making bets. One guy says to Pinto, 'Yeah, he can help ya. What do you need?' He said, 'I'm gonna do a radio show out of my club." This guy said, 'The kid can do it.' I said, 'Yeah, I'll do a radio show.' So Don said, 'I'll bet you on the next fuckin' throw you can't do it.' I said, 'Don't bet your money on the fuckin' throw 'cause you're gonna lose. I can do a radio show from your club.' He rolls, he lost. He didn't get the fuckin' number. So he says, 'Bad day.' I say, 'I'm gonna make it up to you. You're gonna see, I'm gonna do a radio show.' I went up to WCAM in Camden, I said to the general manager there, 'I wanna buy an hour's worth of time. What would it cost me?' He said, 'A hundred dollars.' I said, 'O.K. How long?' He said, 'Thirteen-week contract.' I got him thirteen hundred dollars, and I had the contract. I went back to Don Pinto and his partners at the Venus. I said, 'Look, I'll do an hour's radio show. I want you to give me a hundred and twenty bucks.' I then went out and I sold fifteen minute blocks. Freihoffer Bread, sixty bucks. Crisconi Oldsmobile, sixty bucks. Dale Dance Studio, sixty bucks. Seven-Up, sixty bucks. I made two hundred and forty, and I had a hundred and twenty from the club. Whoever comes through—Tallulah Bankhead, Rocky Graziano—I interview them at the club. Then one day a snowstorm hits the city, closes down the club. I owned the radio time. I had tape to do a show. So I took my records up to Camden and started to play that music. The snow kept coming down, the kids were off from school"—he snaps his fingers: dual double-finger-snaps, the loudest snapping known to man—"and that was that."

So came to be the Geator with the Heater, keeper of the flame and coolest of the cool.

THIRTEEN

Thirty-eight years is a long time, and Blavat and DeMann have seen a lot of things come and go, a lot of things go and come through those years, including themselves, a few times over.

Sitting with the two of them in New York, Freddy after a while seems to slough the skin of Los Angeles, where he has for so long lived and worked. It is as if a breeze from Brooklyn, a breeze of the past, reclaims him. They reminisce about the days gone, and the characters gone.

They were days of naiveté and exuberance: the sweet and celibate two-straws-and-a-milkshake songs of Paul & Paula, the Singing Nun rising to the top of the pop charts. And, beneath it all, as Juggy Gayles had put it: booze, bribes, and broads.

Well, the Singing Nun is gone. She O.D.'d on pills in a suicide pact with another woman in the spring of 1985. But it's not the Singing Nun that these guys miss.

"Yeah, Abner was the best," muses Jerry.

"In New York, when I first broke in, there was a little ring of whores that everyone knew," says Freddy. That was the way it was. Some took their bribery in the currency of flesh, and for others it was both money and broads. "I was always on the look-out, you know, who's gonna hook me up. When I went to Chicago, I got the names of three people to call for whores, and that was mandatory. Well, actually, he gave me one name and he gave me the name of Abner. I went to see Abner, just to say, 'Hi, I'm in town.' And he said, 'O.K., here, you need some whores?' I said, 'Yeah.' 'Here's three, call them and use my name. And meet me every Friday night at the Avenue Hotel. We have a bunch of guys coming around and we all hang out, have drinks; and you look like a cool guy, you can come.' I was white and they were black. I would go every Friday to that Avenue Hotel and, man, I'm telling you"—Freddy shakes his head; there are no words. "Abner drank Johnnie Walker Black straight up, and so I drank Johnnie Walker Black straight up. With a soda chaser."

They're talking about Ewart G. Abner, Jr., who ran Vee-Jay Records, a company that had been founded in Gary, Indiana, in 1953, by Vivian Carter and her companion, James Bracken—Vee for V. Carter, Jay for J. Bracken—and had moved to Chicago in 1954. From the beginning—Vee-Jay's first release, by the Spaniels, a quintet formed at Roosevelt High School in Gary, established the group as one of the leading doo-wop acts of the Midwest—the company was one of the most powerful of independents, strong in the full spectrum of R&B, from the Spaniels to the Dells, and from Jimmy Reed to John Lee Hooker. Under Ewart Abner, who, with the benison of Carter and Bracken, became the guiding force of the label, Vee-Jay, in 1963, became the Beatles' first American label. It was Blavat, the year before, who had convinced Abner that Vee-Jay could prosper with white artists as well as black, bringing him a quartet of Italian-American kids from New Jersey, the Four Seasons, who had a song called "Sherry," which became a Number 1 pop hit *and* a Number One R&B hit for Vee-Jay in 1962.

Abner was so cool that he wore velour jumpsuits while everyone else was wearing suits and ties.

He died two days after Christmas of 1997, age seventy-four. How I would've loved to have had the words of that voice now, so recently but forever, lost. I mean, damn, *velour* jumpsuits.

"I got him to pick up 'Sherry' at the 1962 convention, down in Miami, at the Fountainbleu. Association of Record Merchandisers," says Blavat, "I was with Morris Levy. I bump into Bob Crewe, who I knew forever. He wrote 'Silhouettes.' He says, 'I want you to hear something I just cut with these kids. It's a song called 'Sherry.' I hear it. I said, 'I think this fuckin' thing's a hit.' I play it for Morris; he says, 'That's the worst piece of shit I've ever heard.' I say, 'Crewe, don't get discouraged.' Now, Abner loves me for my ear, O.K.? Between 'He Will Break Your Heart' by Jerry Butler, which I busted wide open for him; between this, that, the other thing—I mean, God gave me an ear. I take Crewe up to Abner's suite, Abner hears it, he says, 'You know, Geator, I think you got something here. But it's a white artist.' I said, 'Abner, who the fuck knows the difference on an acetate or a record if it's white or black? If a hit's a hit, it's got no fuckin' color, man.' They make a deal. I've got this kid with me who works for me in Philly. He's an orphan, maybe fifteen or sixteen years old. Crewe wants to celebrate. I say, 'This kid's never been laid, let's get him a hooker.' I go downstairs. Three hours later, I go back to the room. There's broads and characters all over the place, and there's this kid swapping spits with this fuckin' hooker that's been blowing everybody. He's naked, he's got a sheet around him: it's like a Roman orgy. He says, 'I'm in love.' I said, 'Forget about it.' The kid said, 'Why? She loves me.' I said, 'She's a hooker.' The kid turns white: 'No.' I have a drink in my hand. He spins around, goes to hug me from behind, I go down on the bed, the glass shatters, there's blood all over, the kid faints, they rush me to St. Joseph's. Forty-two stitches."

"It was some convention. I remember there was that pussy-eating contest."

"There was that chubby kid from New York, and this other guy, this local promotion man out of Philadelphia."

"The kid had a robe and came out like a fighter. I don't remember if it was how many they could do, or how long they could do it, or what."

"It was how long it would take for them to get the broads off."

"It was a spectacle. People were laying bets."

Of course, with promotion men involved, suspicions of pay-for-play pseudo-orgasms were not to be dismissed out of hand."

"But I'm telling you," Freddy says, "it had to be for real."

"Yeah, the conventions. Thats where everyone made the deals to get records played."

FOURTEEN

It was a time, all right. But as Heraclitus, the greatest of pre-Socratic promotion men, long ago said: nothing abides.

By 1980, when Freddy was managing Madonna and the gladiatorial cunnilinguists had many years since hung up their robes, the Geator with the Heater seemed down for the count: busted on weapons charges, and then arrested ten months later for allegedly trying to run over a cop who was directing traffic at a road construction site.

They All Sang on the Corner. So the title of a book about doo-wop, written more than a quarter of a century ago, by Philip Groia. It is a title that captures and expresses much. For, from the beginning, rock and roll was of the corner: those four corners of Blavat's youth, and the countless corners of countless youths. Rock and roll, in all its innocence, in all its wickedness, was, from the beginning, of the neighborhood.

And as the Church comprises many churches, so the neighborhood—I can not capitalize that initial *n* no matter how strongly effect and meaning entice me to do so, for, here, to exalt the word would be to misrepresent the thing—comprises neighborhoods beyond number. This is not an idle analogy: the neighborhood is, or was, the embodiment of a spiritual ethos as supernal and puissant in reality as that of the Church in theory. As every neighborhood was a parish, and every parish was a neighborhood, so together they have died.

The true gauge of the freedom of any community is the measurement of the degree of equality by which the fruits of malfeasance are shared by the rulers and the ruled, the cop on the beat and the man or woman on the street. The essence of democracy, as of capitalism, is corruption. Only when the criminal in blue and the criminal in mufti, the peddler and the priest and the alderman and the drunkard—only when they are neighbors of common root and conspiracy is any neighborhood safe for the old lady on the stoop on a hot summer night; only then is there true charity, only then is there a justice that is real, and only then is there life in the air. As the social clubs close, so the churches empty. This is fact, not metaphor.

These may sound to some like words beyond good and evil, but not to one who was to the neighborhood born. Blavat was from the neighborhood. He was from the old school. But the walls of the old school had come tumbling down.

Jerry was doing good, spreading the old-time religion to converts, laying down that lean, mean music to those who had been following him since for years. He was on radio. He was on television. He promoted shows. He had record stores, the Music Museums. The owned a club, Memories, in Margate, New Jersey. Most of his income came from hosting shows—no, hosting is not the right word. The Geator *performed*. I have heard of mercury poisoning. To experience the Geator in action was, and is, to witness what might be called adrenaline poisoning.

Blavat had by no means been the first to prosper by introducing the riches of the R&B past to those who knew them not. As early as 1954, Johnny Belmont of Boston came to Joe Smith of WVDA in that city with the idea of playing obscure R&B records from the years recently past. Smith had given him a half-hour shot on Wednesday nights. The first record Johnny played was "I Smell a Rat," done the year before by Big Mama Thornton, the tough-singing woman whose mean 1953 hit, "Hound Dog," would later be turned into a whimper by Elvis Presley.

"What the hell kind of music is that?" Smith had demanded of Johnny when that first record was played.

"That's rhythm and blues," Johnny had told him.

I'm sitting with Johnny, Peter Wolf, and a few other characters outside Boston, off Route 1, near the Saugus-Lynn line—"Lynn, Lynn, city of sin," as the locals say of this strip of clubs and hot-sheet motels—in a cavernous joint called the Town Line Lounge. "For Your Health & Pleasure," proclaims the Town Line Lounge, "WE SERVE CLEAN AIR! (25 Air Purifiers)." The adjunct Town Line Ten Pin & Billiard Lounge, meanwhile, proclaims: "NEW! ATOMIC BOWLING, IT'S EXPLOSIVE!" Dig it, Jack: if it were happening any more than this, I'd be violating my probation. Johnny, now the proprietor of Cheapo Records in Cambridge, laughs as he looks back to that first Wednesday night a quarter of a century ago, lugging that shopping bag, explaining to a bewildered Joe Smith: "That's rhythm and blues."

Johnny's show took off like wildfire. Joe Smith took to introducing the segment with remarks such as, "Here comes Johnny with his bag of goodies," referring to the shopping bag full of records that Johnny hauled to the studio for each show. Smith in time began using the phrase "oldies and goodies." But it was another disc jockey, Art Laboe of Los Angeles, who came forth with the right preposition: oldies *but* goodies. It was the phrase that stuck, and the title of the successful series of oldies-reissue albums that Laboe inaugurated in 1959.

But the Geator, man, he made the old new, cooler and hipper than the cut of next year's high-roll collar, the fins of next year's Cadillac. He was to every listener what he called every one of them: my *main* man.

"Black night is falling," sang Charles Brown in one of the most chilling and powerful R&B classics, the 1951 hit "Black Night."

Well, black night fell.

"BLAVAT BUSTED," read the headline of a report alleging that the Geator "twice tried to run down a police officer." Blavat had left a Voorhees Township, New Jersey, club with his television crew at about three in the morning of October 4, 1979, when a certain Officer Larry Leaf was directing traffic at a Cherry Hill traffic circle that was partly undergoing construction. According to the report, "Leaf halted Blavat's car, police said, as he attempted to drive on that part of the circle that was being repaved," and when "Leaf asked Blavat for his license, police said, Blavat tried to run the officer down, and then drove around the traffic circle and tried to strike him with his car again."

"GEATOR GAT HEATS N.J. JURY," read the headline of a report that Blavat had been busted, again in Cherry Hill, little more than a month later, on November 8, for "carrying a 'heater,' a slang term for a gun, without a permit." The report stated that, "Besides the .38-caliber revolver Cherry Hill police allegedly found in his car," Blavat "also had in his possession the destructive hollow-nosed bullets only police are sanctioned to use." Reference was made to an earlier weapons charge: "He was placed in a six-month rehabilitation program in Philadelphia in 1976 after firing a bullet into the fender of a car during an argument with an attendant in the basement garage of the apartment building where he then was living."

"Yeah," says Jerry, "I shot that car. "You know why? I pulled into the underground garage, and there's that overhead safety mirror in the corner, and I see these two black cats sneaking round another car, and I just was not in the mood to be robbed. There wasn't any argument.

I just shot, and they fled. I mean, look, would it have been better if I shot them? Would it have been better if I'd let them rob me?"

Slowly, calmly, he goes on. "And I'll tell you about that cop they said I tried to run over. First of all, he was an off-duty cop. He showed no sign of being a cop. He never identified himself as such. He showed no I.D. I found out later that Union Paving had to hire off-duty cops: that was part of the construction deal. But the punchline is, the way this guy asks me to halt is he throws a flashlight at my head. You know the deal. You give some of guy a badge, and..." Jerry's voice trails off mildly, as if there is no reason to reiterate universal truth. "As for trying to run him over, hell, if I were going to do that, I wouldn't have needed a second try."

As for the unlicensed weapon charge, I don't even ask. Any place where the cops have usurped the power of the true protectors of a community—and Cherry Hill until recently had been a peaceful stronghold and the adopted hometown of *i veri* such as Rosario Gambino and others of positions beyond public notice—is a place where arms are justified. Only a fool would rather see hollow-point bullets in the possession of a cop than in that of a real human being with the ways and mores both of neighborhood and church in his blood.

"Look at the record, and you'll see something interesting. I wasn't brought up on any charges until 1981."

FIFTEEN

Angelo Bruno, who had since Jerry's childhood treated him with the love of a father, was murdered on March 21, 1980, reputedly in a killing arranged by his so-called *consigliere*, Antonio "Tony Bananas" Caponigro, who himself did not see the end of that year. Caponigro's naked body, tortured and mutilated, was found in a garbage bag in the South Bronx. Stuck up his dead asshole was a twenty-dollar bill, not quite the desserts of avarice that the decedent had envisioned. Phil Testa, who had overseen this justice, took control, but his rule was not long. In March of 1981, the pieces of him were blown into the street by a remote-control bomb planted in his South Philly home. It was then that Little Nicky Scarfo—who, after stabbing a man to death in a dispute over seating in a restaurant, had been banished by Angelo Bruno to Atlantic

City—seized Philadelphia, which he held until 1991, two years after his conviction for murder had rendered him a lame-duck boss.

The murder of Angelo Bruno was when the walls of the neighborhood came tumbling down.

It was Blavat to whom Bruno's family turned to help keep Bruno's funeral from turning into a media sideshow. With the help of a bunch of his young neighborhood fans, Jerry did his best to keep the television ghouls and their camera crews, the whores of newspaper journalism, and the necrophagous of every kind at bay. Seen with the mourning family during the previous days, the Philadelphia *Daily News* ruminated in print on the eve of the funeral: "How far the Bruno-Blavat friendship goes isn't a matter of public record. But sources say Blavat"—yes, of course, that invisible species, sources, upon which is built all the news that is fit to print—"had been seen on numerous occasions over the last year chauffeuring Bruno around in his Orange Cadillac."

The *Daily News* again, nine weeks after Bruno's casket was laid into the dirt: "John Simone, Angelo Bruno's reputed Trenton numbers overseer, is believed to have taken his place, temporarily, as don of the Philadelphia Mafia family, authorities say." Yes, that most exalted of those spectral "sources," the nebulous "authorities" on high. But Simone had taken nothing, temporarily and otherwise. He was a marked man, a walking corpse, who, for his complicity in Bruno's murder, would soon be discovered in the Staten Island woods with three slugs through the back of his head. Furthermore, "It also was learned that Jerry Blavat, disc jockey and sometime Bruno 'driver,' was subpoenaed to appear before a grand jury investigating the murder."

As Blavat says, *"Look at the record,* and you'll see something interesting."

SIXTEEN

About two weeks after Bruno's funeral, Jerry was in a restaurant when he noticed a familiar-looking man regarding him from the bar: a silent sort of beckoning. Jerry went over to him.

"You know who I am?" the man asked.

"Yes, I do."

"How do you know who I am?"

"Well, I once took Jack Kossman up to Channel 10 when you and he were doing a show on organized crime."

Kossman was the legendary Philadelphia lawyer who had represented Frank Costello among other clients. Jerry had driven Kossman to the television studio at Bruno's request. The panel show, Jerry recalls, was "the usual bullshit."

"You're Edgar Best," Jerry said.

"Yes, I am."

Edgar Best was the head of the Philadelphia

bureau of the F.B.I.

"Let me tell you why I called you over here," Best said. "Your friend that you were very loyal to? I just want to commend you for your stand. He was our friend, too. You're going to get a lot of heat," Best told him, "but I want you to know that he was our friend also."

And the heat did come. "Look at the record..."

It was not until after Bruno's death that Blavat, in February of 1981, was brought to trial for his alleged 1979 "aggravated assault" on the off-duty cop. The only thing that could have made this more bizarre was if he had not been acquitted.

To this day, Jerry is not sure if it originated from federal agents desperately seeking a rat to cast light, no matter how slight, on the baffling tumult that now embroiled the Philadelphia underworld, or from the state of New Jersey, which seemed intent on putting him out of business for motives upon which he can only speculate, involving state officials that cannot here be named.

Years later, when, under subpoena, Jerry appeared before an investigating committee, he discovered only upon his arrival that it was to be a publicized event, a publicity showcase for the committee's political aspirants.

"I said to my lawyers, 'Wait a second, there's nobody around now. Nicky's in jail. They're gonna try to make me look like something. I mean, we've answered all the questions in closed session. Let them take that as a matter of record instead of having my body there.' 'No, they want you.' So I go and, sure enough, there are TV cameras there. I'm sitting with my lawyers, and the U.S. attorney, state of New Jersey, starts, blah, blah, blah. 'Did you know Angelo Bruno?' 'I refuse to answer on the grounds of incrimination, whatever, blah, blah, blah. 'Did you know Carlo Gambino? We have pictures here, blah, blah, blah. Are you a member of organized crime?' I said, 'I refuse to answer that stupid question. I'm taking my Fifth and I'm taking my Amendment privileges, and I'm walking out of here. Anything else?' And I walked out. The only thing they put on television was me walking out, with them saying, 'And this is Blavat's answer." I refused to answer that stupid question. The A.B.C. went after me, tried to revoke my liquor license. Next thing I know, a few years later, they come up with a story that I went to Nicky Scarfo to try to have Hy Lit murdered. This is another attempt to get my liquor license."

Hy Lit is a fellow disc jockey in Philadelphia. Blavat, it was alleged, wanted to rub out the competition.

"I mean, this is insane. Hy Lit thought it was the greatest thing in the world. He called me: 'This is great. Let's do a publicity thing.' I said, 'It's great for you, not for me.' I had to get Nicky Scarfo to testify from prison that I never asked him to get somebody whacked."

That same year, there was a sexual harassment suit filed against him by a fellow worker at the radio station, WPGR, where he was then working.

"There was this black girl, Sharon. She was a sales person. She came to me one day, said she had personal problems, said she needed to make some extra money. I give her a shot at doing this little late-night show, see if she can develop it into something. Roberta Flack, that sort of thing: late-night love songs. The one thing I tell her is that she can't let this interfere with her sales work. Anyway, I discover that she's not following the format for the show, and, besides that, her sales work is going to hell, too. So I set her straight. 'This is all because I'm black,' she says. So she goes to human rights. People know my history. That's that. Then, and I don't know who instigated her, or if anybody instigated her, but next thing I know she leaves and says she's going to get me for sexual harassment."

No small part of this sexual harassment, according to the accusant, consisted of "lewd remarks" such as, "Lady Love, you have a sultry voice; you and I should live together; come live with me." This is the way Jerry talks to waitresses, barely looking at them, as they bring him coffee.

And on, and on, and on. Examining what law-enforcement documents say regarding Blavat's underworld ties, I find, in one government report, a photograph of him walking away from Angelo Bruno as Bruno seems to look disgustedly at the photographer, and, in an F.B.I. report, a Mob turncoat's statement that Blavat had met with De Niro when De Niro wanted to arrange a meeting with Meyer Lansky. What an incriminating encounter, that one, with De Niro, whose criminal career began when he played the Cowardly Lion in a grade-school production of *The Wizard of Oz* and who continued along that yellow brick road of criminality for all the years to follow. Surely the conspiracy of Cowardly Lion, Tin Man, Scarecrow, and Tart would today constitute violation of the RICO Act.

Talking to every survivor of those days of pay-for-play innocence and of experience, of every name bandied about, in malice or in joy or in both, Blavat's is one of the few that remains unsullied. He never took, they say. He was his own man, who had the wits and the ways to make it his way. Even when he brought Crewe and Abner together, bringing about the biggest hit in the history of Vee-Jay, he refused the points that were offered him for "Sherry": a perfectly legitimate and legal offer that he chose simply not to accept.

"That's the difference between you and Dick Clark," said Freddy DeMann when this matter was broached. "He took everything."

Jerry smiled.

Jerry shrugged. "God bless him."

He loved Crewe, he says. He loved Abner. He loved the record. He was making a fortune as it was, he never wanted to be beholden or have his freedom endangered, and that was that.

People in the business envied that freedom, just as men of the old school such as Angelo Bruno respected above all the man who was his own man. It was those who envied who relished and exacerbated the Kafkaesque trials that befell him.

"After I went down, none of these cats were around." He says these words as if there never were a Geator, only that kid from those four corner, moved on now to where the old guys went. But that joint doesn't exist anymore. He nods to himself. "But it was just as good." Then, with a laugh—the Geator's back—"I'm too old to make new friends. I can't even handle the ones that were supposed to be my friends."

Jerry's not down anymore. He brought himself back up, starting over as he had started out after that crap game way back when: buying time, selling blocks on WCAM. Today he's broadcasting over WFIL, he's got a show on WFIL-TV. He's got his club in Margate. That adrenaline is rushing wild as ever. He hosts live shows and what he still calls "record hops," taking down sixteen hundred for weeknight gig, twenty-five, thirty-five hundred for a Saturday night.

If I had half of Freddy DeMann's money, I tell him, I'd burn mine. And yet, sitting there with him, shed of his L.A. skin, the impression is that there were joys back there, in those days before money, that have not returned.

"Phil Kronfeld's men's shop," he recalls wistfully. It was where *la crème de la cool* bought their threads. "I was making fifty dollars a week or something like that, looking through that store window. I dreamed that someday I could afford to go in there and get a suit like the rest of those guys. That sharkskin suit and that silk tie, man. I had to have it. I had to do it."

Blavat has his own wistfulness. I don't even

know if he and DeMann are hearing one another's words, or hearing merely the wistfulness.

"I'm having coffee one morning at my place with Blinky"—he's talking about Blinky Palermo, the Philadelphia-based prince of the fight rackets, under the lordship of Frankie Carbo—"and the phone rings. It's Sinatra. He calls me Matchstick; that's what he always called me. 'Where's the raviolis?' Blah, blah, blah. I said, 'My mother's making the raviolis. There'll be here by six, all right?' So Blinky's with me. He says, 'Who was that?' I said it was Sinatra. He says, 'That bum. I haven't seen him in—.' I said, 'Well, I'm going over with the raviolis and the meatballs and the sausage. Come back at five-thirty, we'll get the limo and we'll go and you'll say hello to Sinatra.' Sure enough, he comes back. we get in the limo with the raviolis, the meatballs, the sausage, and we go see Frankie." For a moment, it's not the past: "Frank loves my mother's meatballs. Because she's *abruzzese*. They're the best cooks."

"Hell," says DeMann, "Later on, when I was a manager, you know how many guys approached me? I remember there was a guy came in with a suitcase full of cash when I represented the Jackson 5. He wanted to be the promoter of a tour the Jacksons were going to do. I said, 'Ah, come on, you're broke. I hear you're broke.' 'Here, here, here'—he's pulling bundles out of the case."

"Was he a successful promoter?" I ask.

"He was. He did Prince. He did a lot of national tours, and then went to jail for tax evasion or something, I don't know."

No, the two of them agree, payola never died. It just became a drag.

"I remember Phil Testa's kid wanted to get into the record business," Blavat says. "They had some kid that they wanted to take into the studio. And they did. They recorded the kid. It was a terrible record. Yeah, Phil's son Salvy, who later got killed. Supposedly by Nicky Scarfo. But I said, 'Salvy, I'm your friend. I'll do anything I can do. But this is the worst piece of shit.' I said, 'Look, a lot of guys, because of who you are, they're gonna say yeah, yeah, yeah, they're gonna play it. But this thing will never sell. It's a piece of shit.' So Phil, his father called me. This was when Ange was still alive. He said, 'Let me tell you something. I wanna thank you for what you told my son. Because we took it to a couple other guys, and they say it's a piece of shit, so I've told him to stay out of it."

"Payola today," says DeMann, "goes on in a much bigger way. Now the stations absolutely hold you up. They're doing a big summer show, or their Christmas show, and it's 'Here's the act we want.' And you better supply them or they won't play your record. They don't say it, but that's what they mean."

Freddy shakes his head, waves aside the present music-business and its million-dollar corporate shakedowns, while Jerry eases back into the days when the racket was exciting. "Who pulled the line, who wasn't gonna pull the line. Who got paid. I'm telling ya, it was incredible. The record business was like a Damon Runyon thing, but with people who knew nothing about the record business."

And all the while, the kids dancing, aswirl, their own pulses singing, never knowing, never hearing, the beat beneath the beat.

"Music was different," says DeMann. "The Mafia was different. There was honor among thieves. Now there isn't any. There's nothing. There's nothing to hang your hat on these days."

SEVENTEEN

Another day. I'm with Wassel, Weiss, and other characters. Freddy is gone back to L.A., but these guys are saying what he said in their own ways.

"Dead, all of it," somebody says.

"They took away the prize."

"Yeah," as Wassel says, intoning agreement with nothing, but merely dismissal. "No more stand-up guys anymore." It is a once common complaint, heard ever more rarely, testimony perhaps of its increasing truth. "This city's dead. This guy, this mayor, this *faccia di morte* here, he's"—the speaker shakes his head, not for want of words, but in disgusted velleity.

He hasn't been to jail in a while. I tell him of an arrest less than a year ago: the first time I was ever in a cell without a single obscenity scrawled on the walls. The walls were filled with only two phrases, in a hundred hands, a hundred intensities: KILL RUDY and DIE RUDY DIE. The notion seems to please all at table, and inspires Wassel to speak again.

"Yeah"—same tone. "People say this guy's like Mussolini. They say he's like Hitler. I tell 'em no. Mussolini and Hitler had friends."

Even Hy Weiss grins. Then he leans forward, softly says:

"You know why the government will never get the music business? It's because they could never understand how it works. And you know why that is? It's because the people in the music business have never understood how it works."

Then Hy Weiss, a boyish gleam in his seventy-six-year-old eyes, returns quite calmly to his eggs and his coffee and his silence.

Torn from the pages of
SAVE THE LAST DANCE FOR SATAN!

The Cascade Records story twin spin six pack, featuring two versions (DJ and stock) of Jack Ruby endorsed '59 killer "Gila Monster"!

NORTON RECORDS AND CURIOS
PO Box 646 Cooper Station, NY NY 10276

Gentlemen, please send me more information about *Giant Gila Monster* Vols. 1 and 2. (Shop on-line at www.nortonrecords.com)

❑ YES! I am interested in these high-quality recordings.

Name _____

Address _____

City _____ Zip _____ State _____

KICKS BOOKS PRESENTS...

Kicks Magazine Rock & Roll Photo Album #1
The Great Lost Photographs of Eddie Rocco

Fabulous collection of previously unpublished photographs by Charlton Publications photographer Eddie Rocco! Sepia-toned trade paperback includes photo tribute to Kicks icon Esquerita plus other favorites including Redd Foxx, Ruth Brown, the Treniers, Jackie Wilson, Johnny Otis, the Beach Boys, Jan & Dean, the Byrds and more!

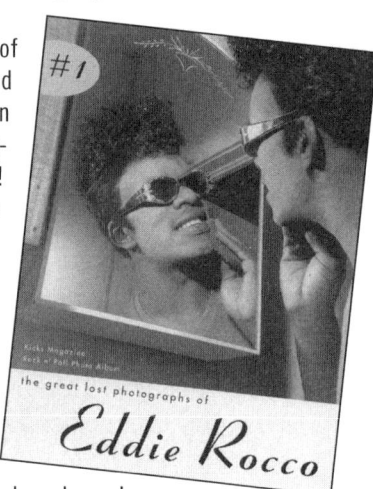

KICKS PUBLISHING CO.
PO Box 646 Cooper Station, NY NY 10276

Gentlemen, I enclose ❑ check or ❑ money order, payment in full for books ordered. I understand that I may be so satisfied, I will need to come back and order more copies. All orders shipped media mail in USA. Foreign orders and others desiring payment via Paypal or credit card, kindly shop online at www.nortonrecords.com.

❑ Rocco book $10 postpaid in USA

Name _____

Address _____

City _____ Zip _____ State _____